Inmate Activity B

Volume 3

Copyright © 2023 by Buttery Branigan Books, 1st edition. All rights Reserved.

No portion of this book may be reproduced in any form without written permission from the publisher or author, except as permitted by U.S. copyright law.

This publication is designed to provide accurate and authoritative information in regard to the subject matter covered. It is sold with the understanding that neither the author nor the publisher is engaged in rendering legal, investment, accounting, mental health or other professional services. While the publisher and author have used their best efforts in preparing this book, they make no representations or warranties with respect to the accuracy or completeness of the contents of this book and specifically disclaim any implied warranties of merchantability or fitness for a particular purpose. No warranty may be created or extended by sales representatives or written sales materials. The advice and stragies contained herein may not be suitable for your situation. You should consult with a professional when appropriate. Neither the publisher nor the author shall be liable for any loss of profit or any other commercial damages, including but not limited to special, incidental, consequential, personal, or other damages.

Cover Art Adobe Stock Author djekill2007 Extended license #317070648
Cover designed by Patricia Branigan
Public Domain Art Work Included courtesy of rawpixel CC0 license

Contact us at: butterybraniganbooks@gmail.com

or visit www.butterybraniganbooks.com to discover

Inmate Activity Book 1

Inmate Activity Book 2

Achieve Success in Recovery

This Activity Book offers a variety of resources aimed at improving your life. It includes mental health support pages, guidance on dealing with problems, processing grief, and managing anxiety. Additionally, an art activity allows you to take a break from your current living situation and envision your ideal home and space. The book also features puzzles to keep your brain sharp and entertain you and a deck of cards with rules for solo and partner card games. You'll find customizable greeting cards to send to your loved ones.

The yoga section of the book introduces movement, encouraging you to utilize your breath and playful spirit as guides. You'll also find captivating works of art to admire, along with beloved images of adorable animals.

Although we designed this book to help you in various ways, it's important to note that not every section will appeal to everyone. Feel free to share the parts that aren't for you and focus on the ones that are.

We value your feedback and encourage you to have your loved ones reach out if there's a specific section of the book you enjoyed or if you have suggestions for our future publications.

At Buttery Branigan Books, we believe everyone deserves joy regardless of circumstances. We aspire to bring light into the darkness of incarceration. We are deeply honored that you have chosen to spend time with our material, and we are grateful for the support of our loyal readers.

We greatly appreciate reviews. Please encourage your loved ones to review this book on Amazon or Barnes and Noble platforms, as reviews help us spread positivity within the prison system.
Please visit **www.butterybraniganbooks.com** for email and links to all our books.

Kindest Regards,
Beth and Patricia

This book belongs to:

Discover Happiness

While finding happiness and joy in prison may pose challenges, it is not impossible. Here are some scientifically supported methods to enhance your well-being even within the confines of prison.

1. Discover the meaning and purpose of your life and engage in activities that support that meaning or purpose. Complete your education, write a novel, experiment with your artistic skills, etc.

2. Build positive relationships with other inmates, staff members, and your loved ones on the outside.

3. Practice gratitude. Focus on the positive things in your life. They might be small, like a good snack or meal, or more significant, like your health or relationships.

4. Take care of your physical health by exercising and trying to get enough sleep.

5. Seek out support. Use your prison's services if you are struggling with your mental health. Talk with a counselor, attend group meetings or church services.

6. Try a mindfulness practice such as meditation or deep breathing. If you are feeling anxious, try the grounding exercises in this book.

Attaining happiness in prison may require effort, but it is possible. By focusing on things within your control and taking proactive steps, you can enhance your level of happiness.

I Can Discover Happiness

Steps I can take to discover meaning or purpose for my life:

____

____

____

____

____

Positive people in my life:

____

____

Things I am grateful for:

____

____

____

____

My support system includes the following:

____

____

____

____

My mindfulness practice includes the following:

____

____

____

____

____

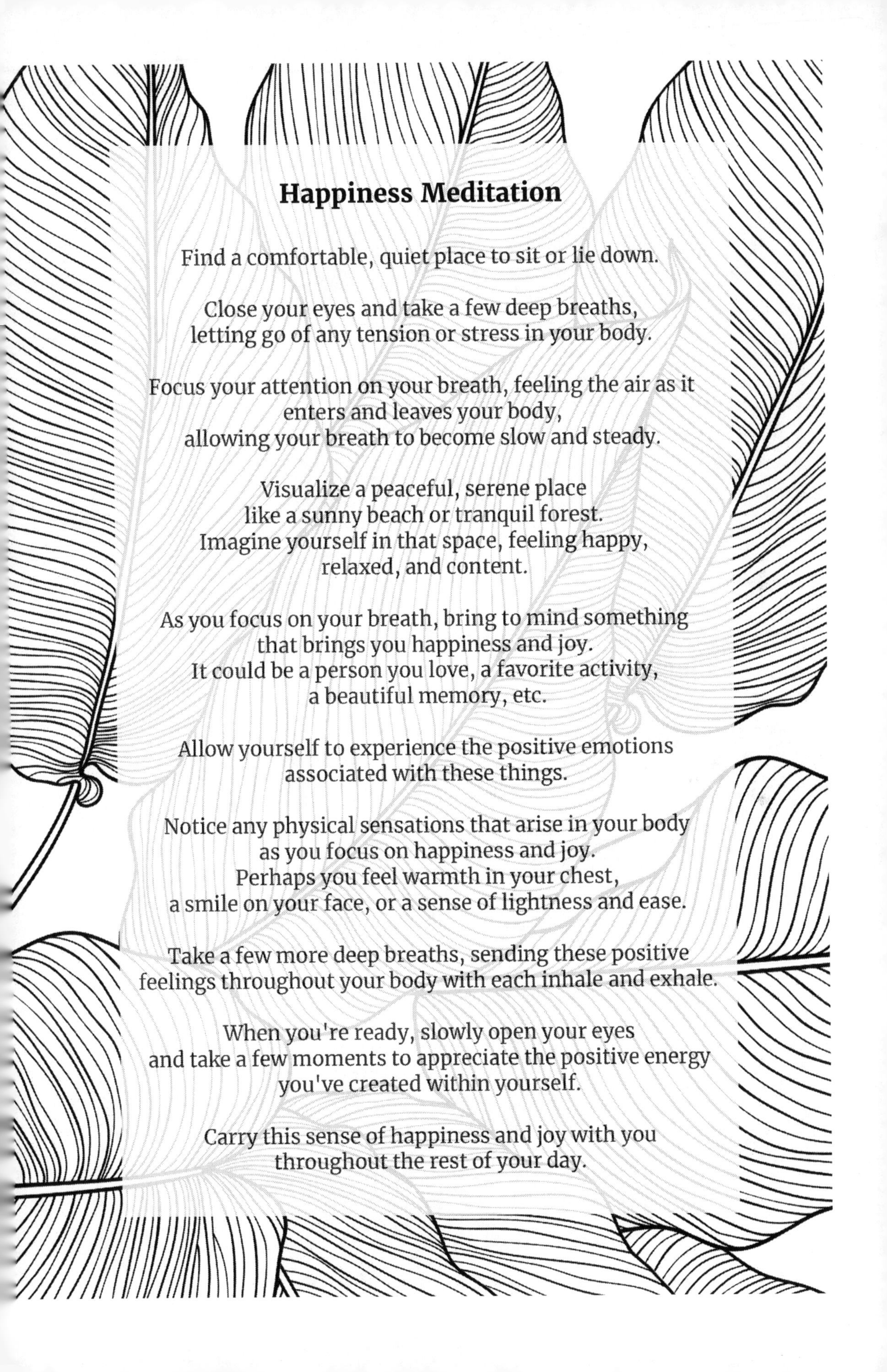

Happiness Meditation

Find a comfortable, quiet place to sit or lie down.

Close your eyes and take a few deep breaths,
letting go of any tension or stress in your body.

Focus your attention on your breath, feeling the air as it
enters and leaves your body,
allowing your breath to become slow and steady.

Visualize a peaceful, serene place
like a sunny beach or tranquil forest.
Imagine yourself in that space, feeling happy,
relaxed, and content.

As you focus on your breath, bring to mind something
that brings you happiness and joy.
It could be a person you love, a favorite activity,
a beautiful memory, etc.

Allow yourself to experience the positive emotions
associated with these things.

Notice any physical sensations that arise in your body
as you focus on happiness and joy.
Perhaps you feel warmth in your chest,
a smile on your face, or a sense of lightness and ease.

Take a few more deep breaths, sending these positive
feelings throughout your body with each inhale and exhale.

When you're ready, slowly open your eyes
and take a few moments to appreciate the positive energy
you've created within yourself.

Carry this sense of happiness and joy with you
throughout the rest of your day.

The Scream: Edvard Munch

Distress-Tolerance Skill: Self-Calming

When you're feeling overwhelmed or anxious,
try using this self-calming skill. It involves paying
attention to what you see, hear, smell, taste, and touch,
which can help you comfort and calm yourself.
This technique can reduce the intensity of your emotions.

Sight:

- Surround yourself with things that you like to look at. Find your favorite animal or art scene from this book and display it in your space.
- Read a book, or watch a TV show you enjoy.

Sound:

- Listen to calming music or sing a favorite song.
- Try to create an instrument in your space. Drum on the wall or tap your feet to a rhythm to make music any way you can.

Touch:

- Massage your feet, hands, or the back of your head.
- Touch objects in your cell. Are they cold, soft, textured, etc?

Taste:

- Enjoy a favorite food or drink.
- Savor the taste and take your time eating or drinking.

Smell:

- Find something in your space that smells nice.
- Smell one of your snacks before eating and see if it brings comfort.

Lying, Negative, Automatic Thoughts

Everyone has negative thoughts that randomly come to their minds. But if you notice them, you can question them and make sure they're not deceiving you. Once you realize how your negative thoughts affect you, you can replace them with more realistic ones. Here's a worksheet that can help you challenge your negative thoughts. Begin with the example provided and then move on to your own thoughts.

1. Describe in detail what happened. Be specific as possible, even if you messed up.

   I burned my fingers when I touched a hot pan in the kitchen without using an oven mitt.

2. How did you feel about what happened?

   I feel stupid that I made such a dumb mistake.

3. What is the evidence that supports your negative thought?

   I **was stupid because I knew the pan was hot and touched it anyway.**

4. What is the evidence that your negative thought is not the truth?

   I was in a hurry and trying to do too much at once. I am usually very smart when I cook and rarely get hurt.

5. What is an alternative thought based on reality?

   I was trying to do too much at once. I need to slow down and take my time.

6. How does the more accurate thought make you feel?

   I feel a little mad that I got burned, but I know it was a mistake, and mistakes happen.

Try challenging your own negative automatic thoughts on the provided sheet.

1. Describe in detail what happened. Be specific as possible, even if you messed up.

2. How did you feel about what happened?

3. What is the evidence that supports your negative thought?

4. What is the evidence that your negative thought is not the truth?

5. What is an alternative thought based on reality?

6. How does the more accurate thought make you feel?

Affirmations

Positive affirmations are powerful statements that can change your mindset and make you feel better about yourself. Here are some helpful tips to make the most of positive affirmations.

Base your affirmation on facts:

Be aware of your positive feelings throughout the day and say a positive affirmation to go with that feeling. You should repeat a declaration of *I am calm* when you feel relaxed. If you are happy, repeat something like, *I am content,* to reaffirm how you truly feel to your brain.

Tailor your affirmations to suit yourself:

If you are trying to achieve a goal, create an affirmation that goes along with your work, such as, *I am working on reacting positively in situations.* Repeat this as you work toward your goal.

Believe in your affirmation:

Even in prison, you can feel peaceful. You can find joy and happiness by paying attention to the good moments and being aware of them. When you stay focused on the present moment, you'll notice more of these positive experiences in your life.

Try a breathing exercise or grounding technique along with your affirmation. Adding these extra steps will help your mind and body believe what you tell your brain. They will help you become a person who seeks and finds positive things in your life.

My Affirmations

I am strong enough to endure this challenge.

I am worthy of forgiveness and redemption.

I have the power to create a better future for myself.

I seek joy, and I find it.

I am capable of learning and growing from my mistakes.

I am loved and supported by my family and friends.

I am making progress toward my goals every day.

I can turn my life around and positively impact the world.

I choose to focus on positivity and hope for the future.

I am a valuable human being with unique talents and abilities.

My past mistakes do not define me, and I have the power to create a new future for myself.

I am resilient and can overcome any obstacle that comes my way.

I am worthy of love and respect both from others and myself.

I am calm.

I am grateful for the lessons this experience taught me and will use them to better myself.

I am at peace.

I am capable of forgiveness for myself and for others who have wronged me.

I will focus on the present moment and make the most of my time.

My Affirmations

Grief and Loss

Grief and loss are unavoidable. You might experience the loss of someone important to you, lost time with family and friends, or your freedom.

Loss and grief are closely intertwined. They can bring intense distress, affecting both your physical and emotional well-being.

Look at the drawing on the next page. Each square represents a different phase of grief. The pain button symbolizes discomfort. The ball symbolizes your grief. When you experience a loss, the ball is large, causing suffering as it constantly hits the pain button.

As time goes by, the ball of grief will shrink. As it bounces around your life, it will hit the pain button less, but each time it makes contact with the button, you will still experience pain.

As more time passes, the ball of grief will become smaller. It won't hit the pain button as often, but when it does, you will still feel the pain of the loss.

When you go through grief and loss, it can change your life. It's important to give yourself enough time to handle the emotions you're experiencing. You can use the following page to help you work through those emotions connected to your grief and loss.

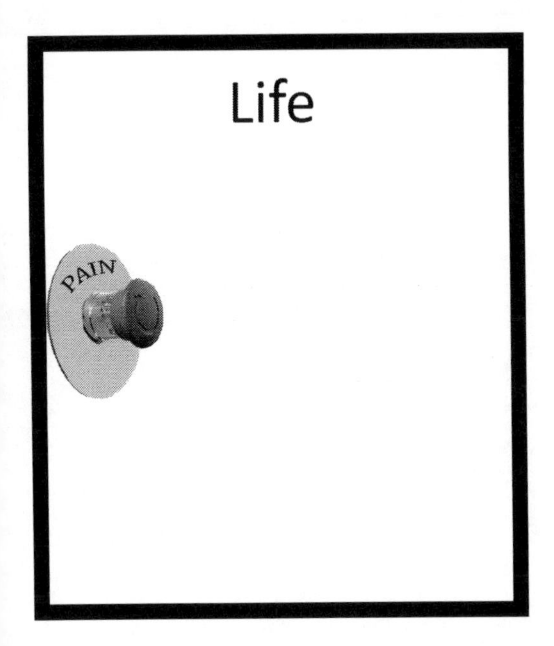

Life before grief

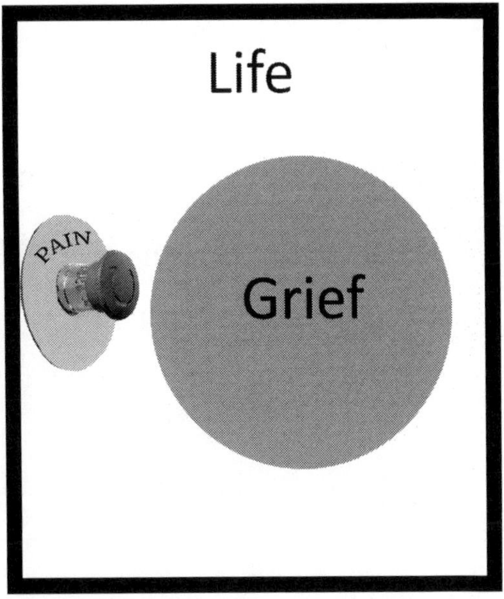

When first faced with grief, your ball of grief is large. Therefore, it hits the pain button consistently.

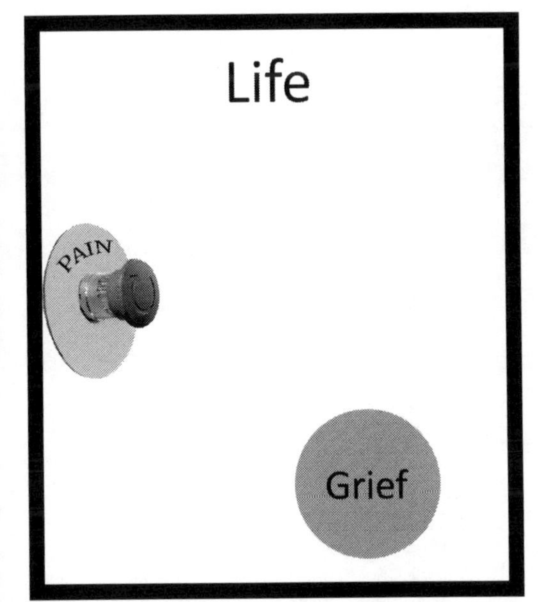

As life goes on, the ball of grief will shrink. It will still hurt when the ball of grief hits the pain button.However, because the ball is smaller, it will hit less often.

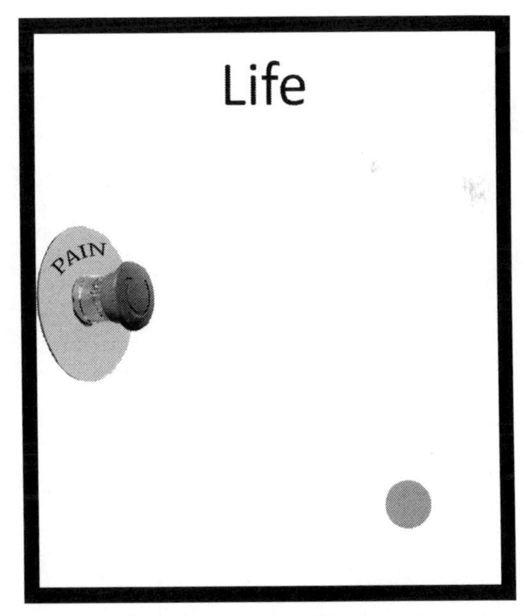

The ball of grief will continue to shrink with time. It will still hurt when it hits the pain button but will hit even less often.

My Grief Plan

What can I do to take care of myself while I'm grieving?

Who can I speak with to help me deal with my emotions?

Is there a memory I can think of to help me in this moment?

Why is it important for me to deal with my loss and grief in a healthy manner?

Where can I get additional support?

Grief Meditation

Sit or lay in a comfortable space.
Take several deep breaths relaxing your jaw, forehead, shoulders, and entire body without judgment.
Repeat the following:

I honor this loss in my life.
I allow myself to grieve.
Take two deep breaths and take a moment to feel your emotions.

I honor the joyful past.
I celebrate the memories I have.
Take two deep breaths and take a moment to appreciate a memory.

I honor the pain that is left behind.
I offer myself compassion for all that I am feeling.
Take two deep breaths and take a moment to give yourself a word of encouragement.

I honor the imperfectness of my relationship that is lost.
I offer myself forgiveness.
Take two deep breaths and offer yourself forgiveness.

I honor my body while I grieve.
I offer myself rest and grace.
Take two deep breaths and allow your body to relax.

I honor my mind while I grieve.
I offer myself loving-kindness.
Take two deep breaths and wrap yourself in a gentle hug.

I accept that my grief will lessen over time, but my loss will not.
Take several deep breaths and relax your entire body.

Exercises to Ease Anxiety

Everyone responds differently to anxiety.
These exercises will help you discover which tool works best for you.

#1

- Find a comfortable sitting position and ensure your spine is straight.
- Roll your shoulders back and down to create length in your neck.
- Slowly turn your neck to the right, looking over your shoulder. Hold for 10 to 20 seconds, then return to center.
- Slowly turn your neck to the left, looking over your shoulder. Hold for 10 to 20 seconds, then return to center.
- Interlace your fingers with your thumbs facing downward. Place your hands behind your head, ensuring your shoulders are broad and your thumbs rest on your neck.
- Focus your gaze to the right, moving only your eyes (do not turn your head). Hold this position for 30 to 60 seconds until you yawn or take a deep breath.
- Shift your gaze to the left, again moving only your eyes. Hold for 30 to 60 seconds until you yawn or take a deep breath.
- Remove your hands from behind your head and slowly turn your whole head to the right and then to the left.
- Notice your neck's increased range of motion and pay attention to how you feel.

#2

Progressive Muscle Relaxation (PMR)

- Tense and then relax all of your muscles one group at a time. Begin with your feet.
- Tense the muscles as much as you can and hold for 10 seconds.
- Release.
- Move to your legs.
- Continue up the body focusing on one body part at a time.
- After you have tensed and relaxed each part of your body, try tensing and relaxing your whole body at once.
- Take several deep breaths, in through your nose and out through your mouth.

#3
Butterfly Tapping

- Find a comfortable sitting or lying position.
- Position your hands, palms facing your body, on your chest, with your thumbs crossing and your fingers pointing upwards.
- Tap your fingers, alternating between one hand and the other.
- While tapping, pay attention to your breath, taking deep breaths.
- Continue this rhythm for several minutes.

#4

- Take a deep breath, filling your belly with air.
- Hold for one second.
- Take another breath in without releasing the first breath.
- Hold for one or two seconds.
- Release your breath in one long exhale.

#5

- Choose a comfortable sitting or lying position.
- Straighten your spine and roll your shoulders down.
- Wrap your arms around yourself, placing your hands on your upper arms below the shoulders. Feel free to experiment with which arm is on top.
- Tap one side of your arm and then the other, creating a rhythmic pattern from side to side.

*For a challenge: take deep breaths as you tap. Employ shorter breath intakes, a momentary break, and lengthier breath releases.

#6
Nostril breathing

- Use a finger to block one of your nostrils.
- Inhale and exhale ten times only using one nostril
- Switch to block the other nostril.
- Inhale and exhale ten times only using that nostril.

*For a challenge: breathe in through one nostril and out through the other.

A Meditation to Quiet Anger

Find a quiet, peaceful place to sit comfortably
without distractions.

Take a few deep breaths and allow your body to relax,
focusing on your breath and letting go of any tension.

As you settle into this state of relaxation, think about the
source of your anger without judgment or blame,
simply recognizing that it exists within you.

Imagine the anger as a small flame burning
within your chest.

Visualize yourself watching the flame, allowing it to burn,
not adding fuel to the fire.

As you observe the flame, begin to detach yourself from it.

The flame is in you but not a part of you.
See it as separate from you, and imagine it gradually
shrinking and fading away.

Picture yourself feeling lighter and more at
ease as the anger dissipates.

Repeat a calming phrase to yourself.

I am at peace, or I can let go.

Focus on the sound and vibration of the words,
allowing them to soothe and calm you.

Take a few more deep breaths while feeling gratitude
for your efforts.

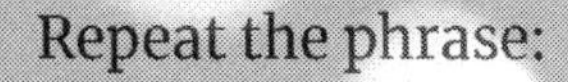

Repeat the phrase:

I am happy I am doing the work to find peace.
I will experience joy.

Take several deep breaths.

Wrap your arms around yourself in a hug.

You have the power to control your anger.
Recognize that anger is a natural part of being human,
but it doesn't have to control you.
You can learn to let go of anger and find peace
within yourself with practice.
Dealing with anger is a process;
developing this skill takes time and patience.
Be gentle with yourself and continue practicing these
meditation techniques whenever you feel anger rising.
With persistence, you can cultivate a sense of calm
and inner peace that will serve you well.

Challenge Negative Thoughts with the Four P's

Review each P factor and answer the questions below to help challenge negative thought patterns.

Personalize: Is it all about me?

- What evidence is there that this situation is not entirely my fault?
- What role did other people or external factors play in this situation?
- How would I advise a friend who was in a similar situation as me?

Permanent: Is this going to last forever?

- Is this situation permanent, or is it temporary?
- What steps can I take to improve this situation?
- Have you experienced positive changes in the past that you once thought were permanent?

Prevalent: Is my whole life affected?

- Is this situation affecting every area of my life or just a few?
- What positive aspects in my life has this situation not impacted?
- What actions can I take to improve other areas of my life affected by this situation?

Powerless: Do I control any part of the situation?

- What aspects of this situation can I control?
- What steps can I take to improve this situation, even if I cannot control all aspects of it?
- Can I use external resources or support systems to help me feel more in control?
- What positive steps can I take to help me feel more empowered in this situation?

Keep in mind that it takes time and practice to challenge negative thoughts. Regularly writing down your responses and reviewing them can reinforce positive changes in your thinking.

Personalize: Is it all about me?

____

____

____

____

Permanent: Is this going to last forever?

____

____

____

____

Prevalent: Is my whole life affected?

____

____

____

____

Powerless: Do I control any part of the situation?

____

____

____

____

Feel Your Feelings

In prison, you may feel like you have to keep your emotions to yourself. As a result, you might resort to harmful actions to hide or cope with your feelings.

Keep in mind that emotions are temporary. When you feel happy or content, pause and appreciate those positive feelings. On the other hand, if you're experiencing sadness or anger, remind yourself that these emotions will pass with time.

Take a few minutes to sit quietly and experience the emotions you usually try to avoid.

Take a couple of deep breaths and repeat this meditation:

I am okay.
I have emotions.
All of my emotions are okay.
All emotions will pass.
I am okay.

Take a couple more deep breaths.

When your emotions become too much to handle, sharing your feelings with someone can help. Utilize the mental health supports that might be available to you. If that is not an option and you feel unstable, you can try different exercises to reduce anxiety. This book has some helpful techniques, or you can try writing in a journal or looking at calming images while taking deep breaths. Imagine yourself in a happy and safe place, allowing your mind to take a break.

End-of-Day Meditation

Today is over.
I can not relive today.
I can not change what happened today.
I can learn from my mistakes.
I can celebrate my success.

I move forward.
I leave today behind.

Tomorrow is a new day with new challenges.
I will greet tomorrow when it arrives in the morning.
The only thing left for me to do today is to rest.
I will rest my mind.
I will rest my body.

I move forward.
I leave today behind.

Tense and relax all areas of your body, starting with your feet.
Repeat the following phrase as you move upwards and relax each area of your body:

I desire to rest.
I move forward.
I leave today behind.

Take several deep breaths through your nose and slowly out your mouth sending healing breath and love to your body.

The Starry Night: Vincent van Gogh

Yoga

Yoga

Yoga is a highly beneficial exercise for both physical and mental well-being. It enhances muscle tone, improves flexibility, and promotes mental health through breath control during poses.

If you don't have a yoga mat or soft surface to practice on, you can use a mattress to cushion your body. If this option is unavailable, focus on standing poses to avoid pain or injury on a hard surface. Yoga should not be painful. If you experience pain, take a break or try a different pose.

Warm-up: Begin your yoga session with a few minutes of gentle stretching and deep breathing.

Set your intention: It could be anything from finding peace and relaxation to improving flexibility or building strength. (An intention can start with, "I choose ...")

Practice proper alignment: Pay attention to your body's alignment in each pose. Align your head, neck, and spine, and distribute your weight evenly.

Breathe deeply: Focus on deep, controlled breathing. Inhale deeply through your nose, expand your belly, and exhale fully through your nose or mouth.

Start with foundational poses: Begin with basic poses such as Mountain Pose (Tadasana), Child's Pose (Balasana), Downward Facing Dog (Adho Mukha Svanasana), and Warrior Poses (Virabhadrasana). These poses build strength, balance, and flexibility.

Progress gradually: Introduce more challenging poses as you become more comfortable with the foundational poses. Listen to your body, and don't force yourself into uncomfortable or painful positions.

Maintain a steady practice: Consistency is key. Aim to practice yoga regularly, whether daily or a few times weekly. Regular practice helps you progress and experience the full benefits of yoga.

End with relaxation: After physical practice, allow yourself time for relaxation. End your session with Corpse Pose (Savasana), lying flat on your back, and focus on deep relaxation and letting go of any tension.

If possible, consult with a qualified yoga instructor or attend classes to ensure proper form and guidance, especially if you're new to yoga. Enjoy your practice, and have fun exploring the wonderful world of yoga!

Yoga Foundational Poses

Sun Salutation

1. **Pranamasana (Prayer Pose)**: Stand at the front of your mat, feet together or hip-width apart, and bring your palms together in front of your heart center. Take a moment to center yourself and connect with your breath.
2. **Tadasana (Mountain Pose)**: Stand with your feet a comfortable distance apart, arms at your side. Lengthen your spine, engage your core, and ground down through your feet. Keep your gaze forward.
3. **Urdhva Hastasana (Upward Salute)**: Exhale and gently arch your upper body backward, keeping your arms alongside your ears and palms pressed together. Lift your head and look up if comfortable.
4. **Uttanasana (Forward Fold)**: Inhale and hinge forward at the hips, bringing your torso toward your legs. Allow your hands to come down to the mat beside your feet or rest them on your shins. Relax your head and neck, and aim to bring your chest closer to your thighs.
5. **Ardha Uttanasana (Halfway Lift)**: Exhale and place your hands on your shins or fingertips on the mat. Lengthen your spine, lift your chest, and gaze forward. Keep your legs active and your core engaged.
6. **Chaturanga Dandasana (Four-Limbed Staff Pose)**: Step back to a high plank position as you exhale. Lower your body, keeping your elbows close to your sides and at a 90-degree angle. Your shoulders should align with your elbows.
7. **Bhujangasana (Cobra Pose)**: Inhale, press your palms into the mat, straighten your arms, and lift your chest off the ground. Keep your pelvis and lower body engaged with the mat, and draw your shoulder blades toward each other.
8. **Adho Mukha Svanasana (Downward-Facing Dog)**: Exhale and lift your hips up and back, coming into an inverted V shape. Press your palms into the mat, lengthen your spine, and engage your core. Relax your heels toward the ground, but it's okay if they don't touch.
9. **Ardha Uttanasana (Halfway Lift)**: Inhale and return to the halfway lift position, lengthening your spine and bringing your hands to your shins or fingertips to the mat. Keep your gaze forward.
10. **Uttanasana (Forward Fold)**: Exhale and fold forward
11. **Urdhva Hastasana (Upward Salute)**: Inhale, sweep your arms out to the sides and overhead, and rise to stand. Bring your palms together and gently arch backward.

YOGA
Sun Salutation A
Pranamasana 1
Tadasana 2
Urdhva Hastasana 3
Uttanasana 4
Ardha Uttanasana 5
Chaturanga Dandasana 6
Bhujangasana 7
Adho Mukha Shvanasana 8
Ardha Uttanasana 9
Uttanasana 10
Urdhva Hastasana 11

7
YOGA FOR
BALACNE
Half Splits II
Half Boat
Tiger
Tree with Arms Up
Standing Splits
Warrior III with Prayer Hands
Lord of the Dance

Goddess

10 YOGA *for* MUSCLE BURNING

Side *plank*

Plank *upward*

wheel

Revolved *Chair*

Low *lunge*

Boat

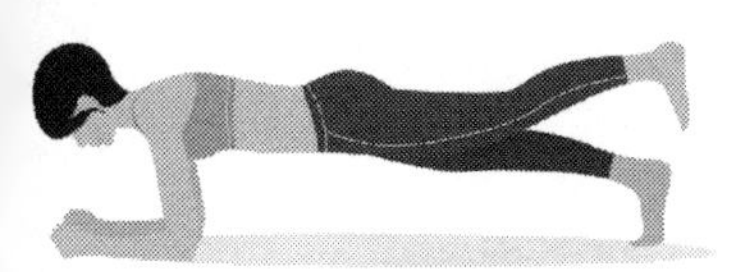

One *leg plank*

Side *crane*

Extended *locust*

8 YOGA TO MOVE THE BODY

Horizon Lunge

Side body Stretch

Downward-Facing Dog

Crescent Lunge on the Knee with Arms Extended

Standing Forward Bend

Crescent Lunge on the Knee with Cactus Arms

Bridge

Extended Child

YOGA For POSTURE

Cow Face Forward Bend

Camel

Bridge

Downward-Facing Dog

High Cobra

Full Plank

Bow

Warrior I

Wide Legged Forward Bend

YOGA for STRONG ARMS & CORE

Single Arm Full Plank

Dolphin

Upward-Facing Dog

Downward-Facing Dog with Knee

Side Dolphin Plank

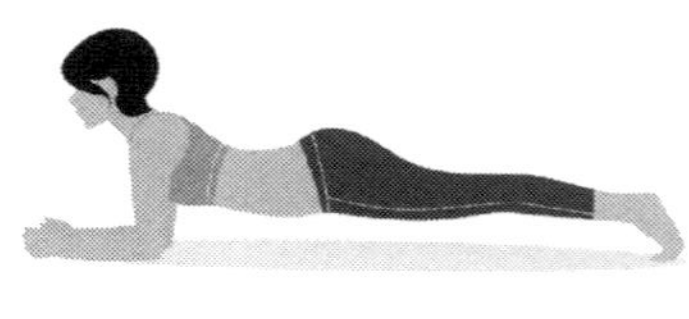

Dolphin Plank

Downward-Facing Dog

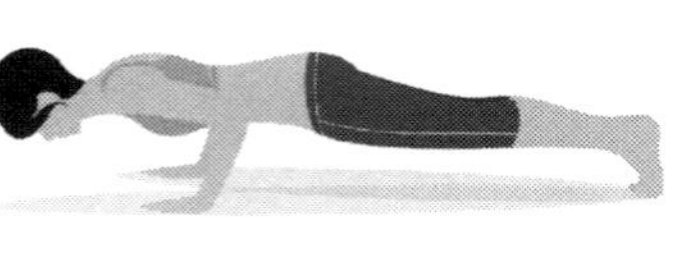

Low Plank

Downward-Facing Dog

Downward dog hand to ankle

Plank with Knee to Opposite Tricep

Revolved Crescent Lunge

YOGA For DETOXIFYING

Wide Legged Forward Bend I

Sage Marichi's III

Twisted Roots

One Legged Wind Removing

Head to Knee

10
Best Poses to Get
Strong Hips
Crescent Lunge
Crescent Lunge Twist
Awkward
Goddess
Crescent Lunge Forward Bend
Happy Baby
Side Lung
Garland
Goddess Twist
Cradle Baby

Infographic
YOGA
Poses
10
Eight *Angle*
Crescent Lunge with Prayer Hands
Wide *Child's*
One Legged Downward *Facing Dog*
Crescent Lunge *Forward Bend*
Bound *Revolved Chair*
Revolved Crescent Lunge *with Extended Arms*
Bound Revolved *Crescent Lunge*

American Gothic: Grant Wood

Art Activity

Use the following outlines of rooms to decorate as you would like. Use shading, patterns, and colors to make the space reflect your style.

Add animal, plant, and people templates representing your interests and personality to make your room more personalized.

When your drawings are complete, you can use them while you meditate. Travel to your decorated rooms in your mind to find peace and calm in your day.

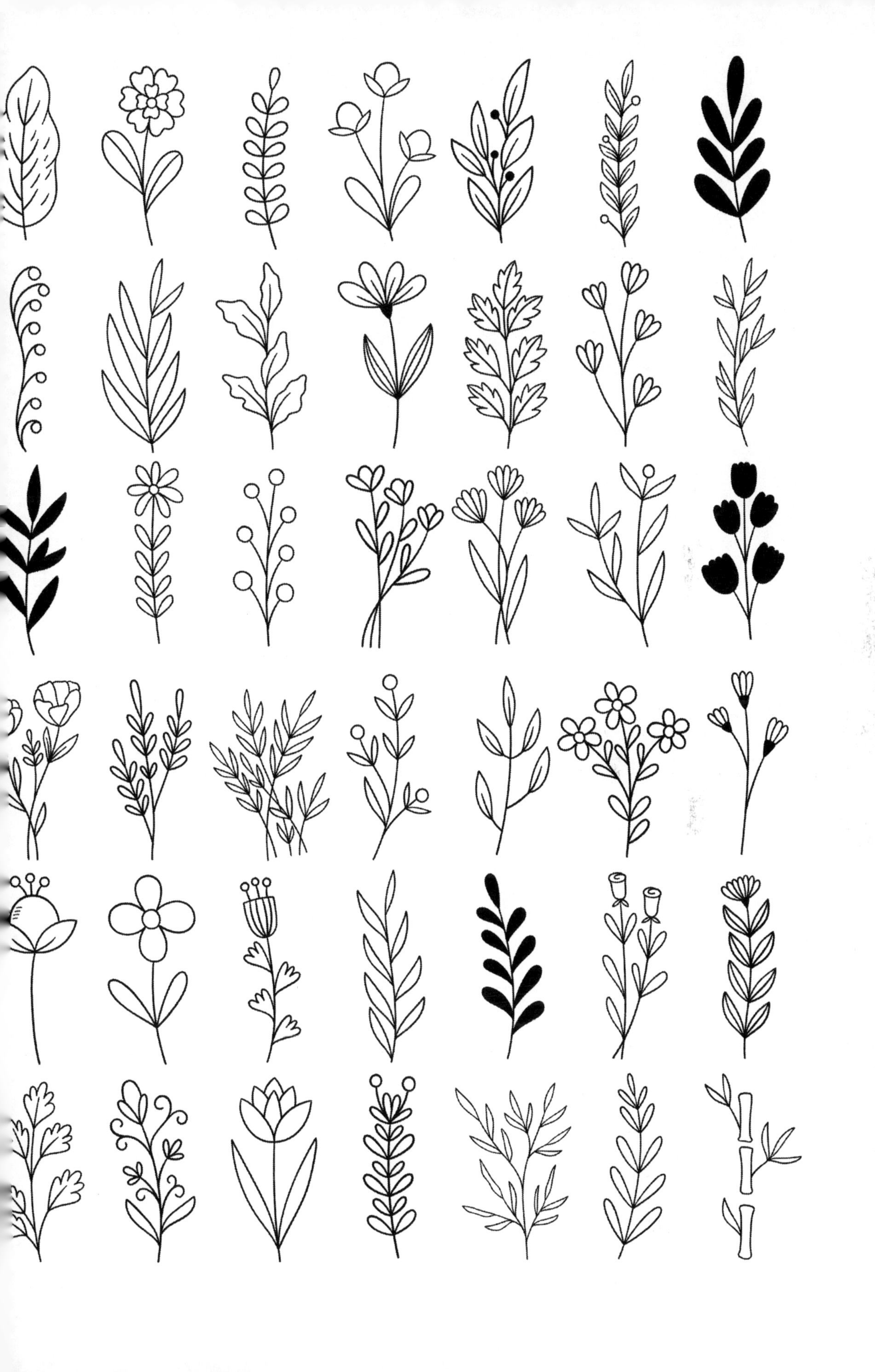

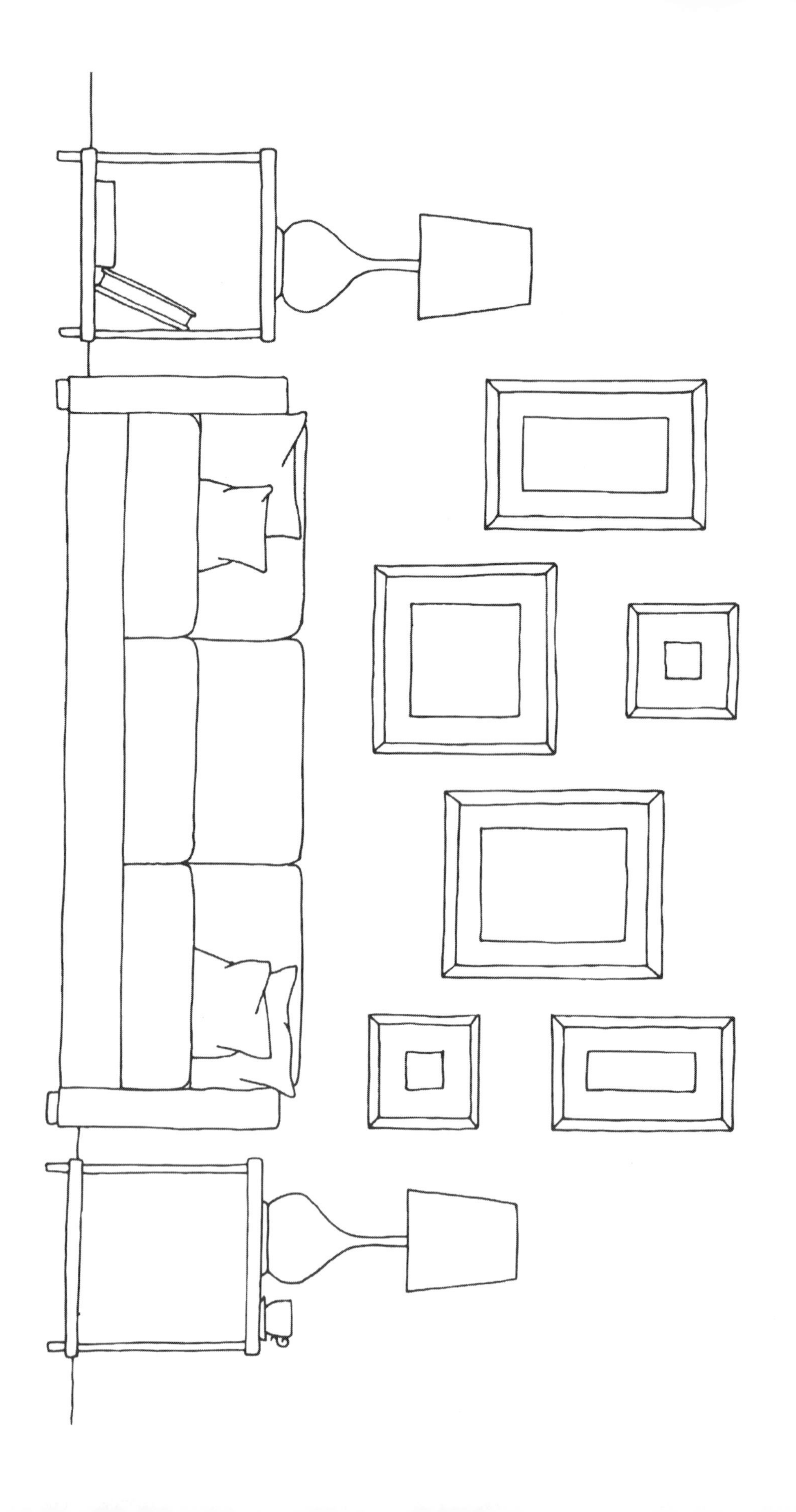

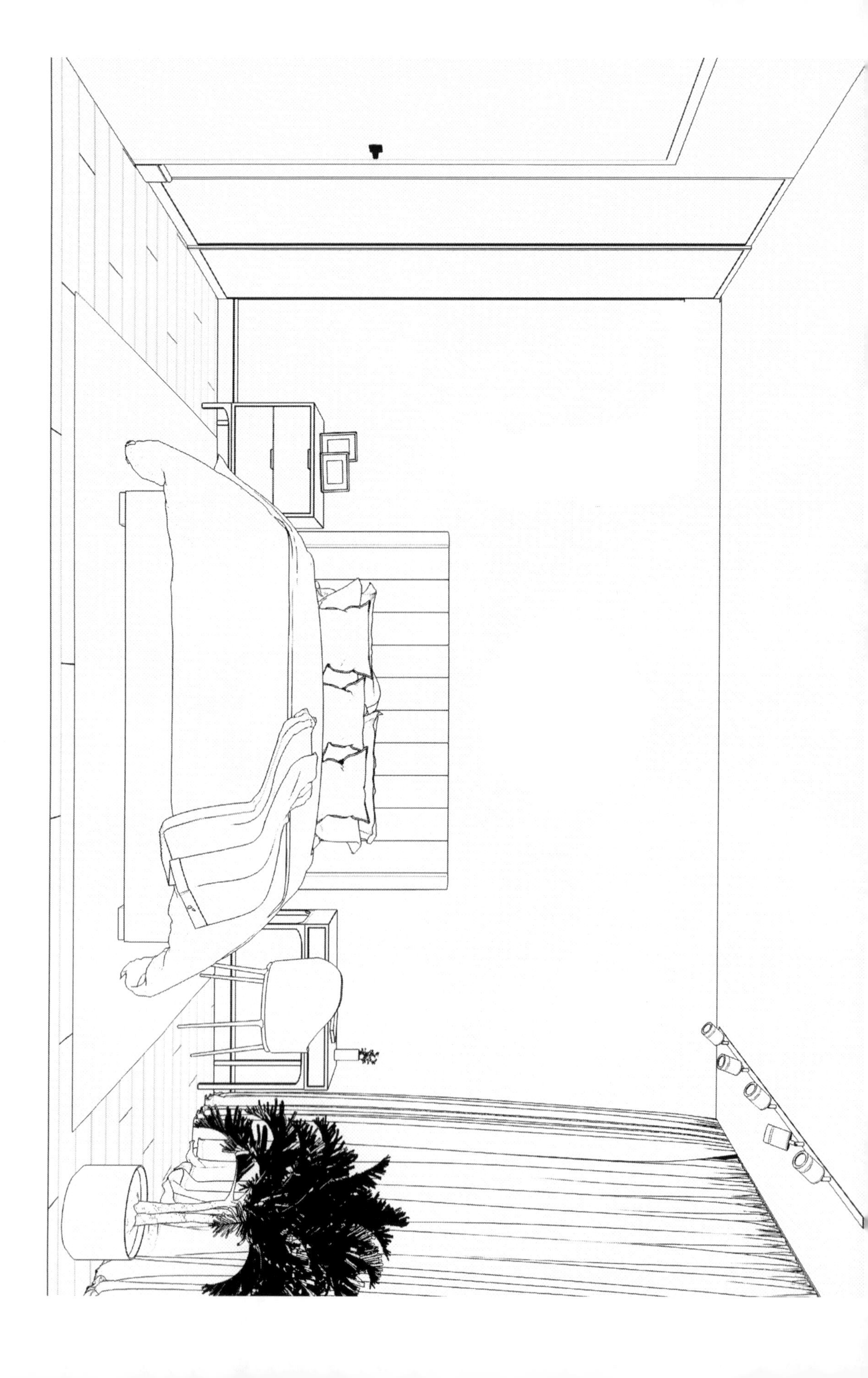

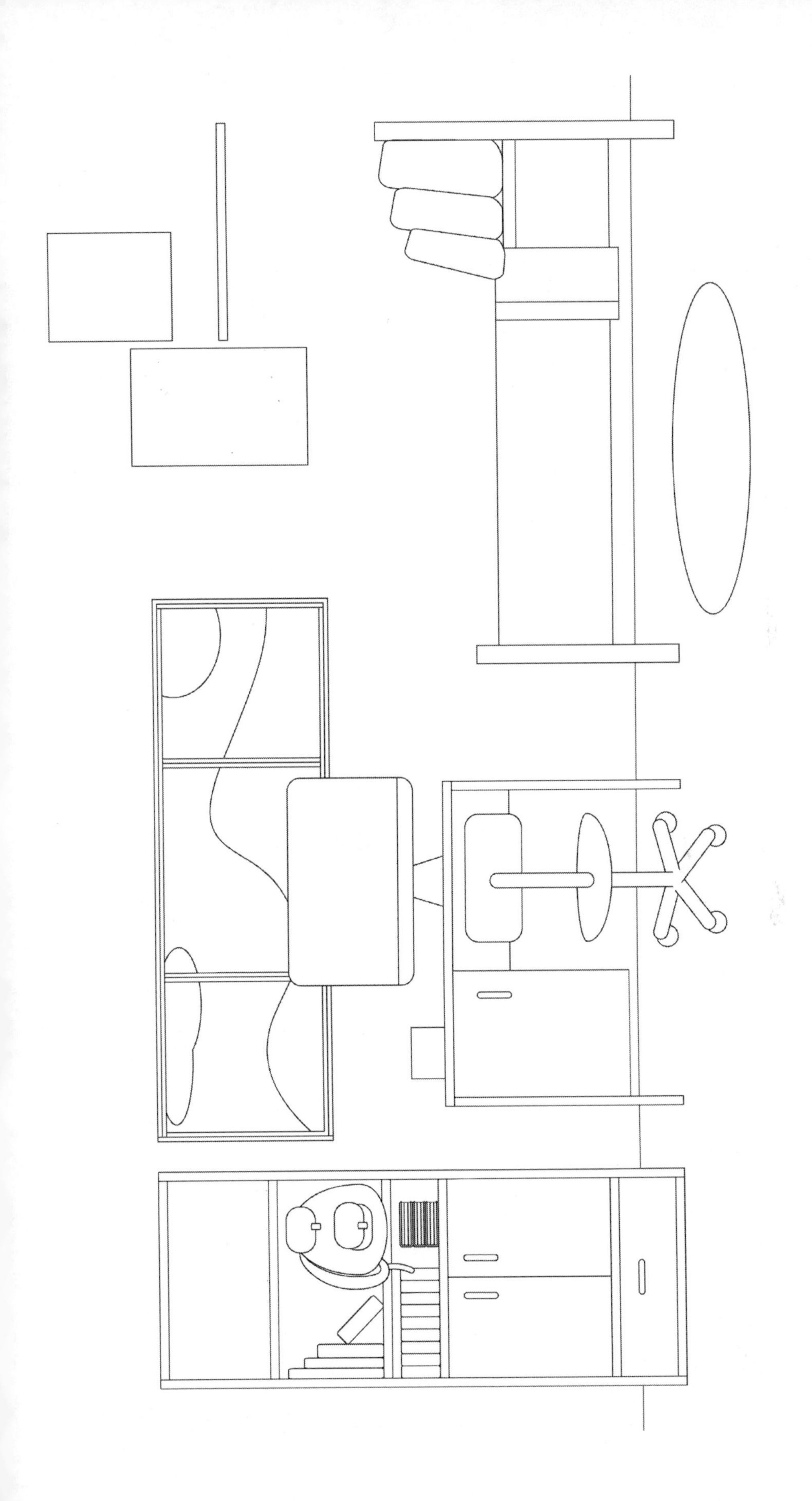

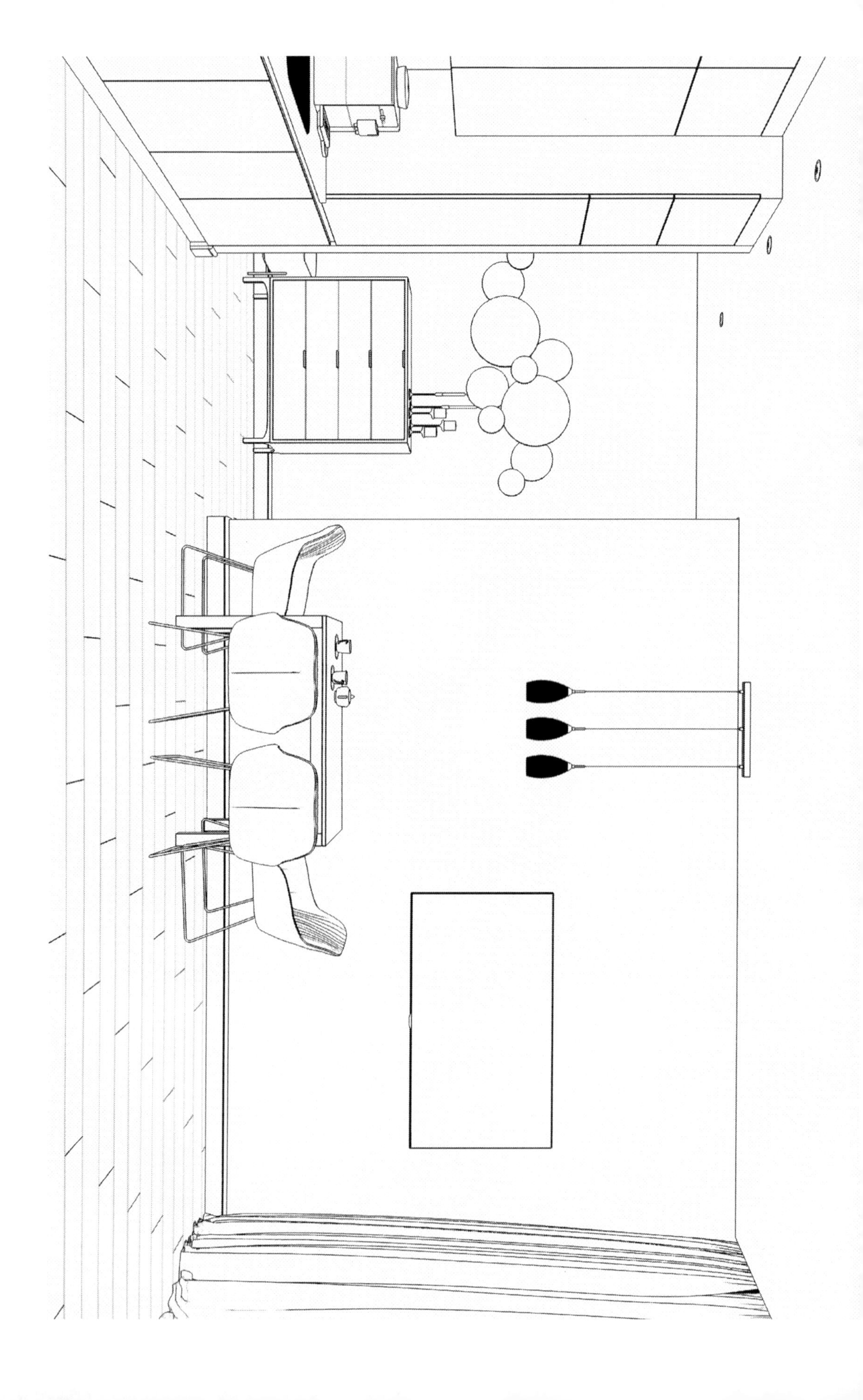

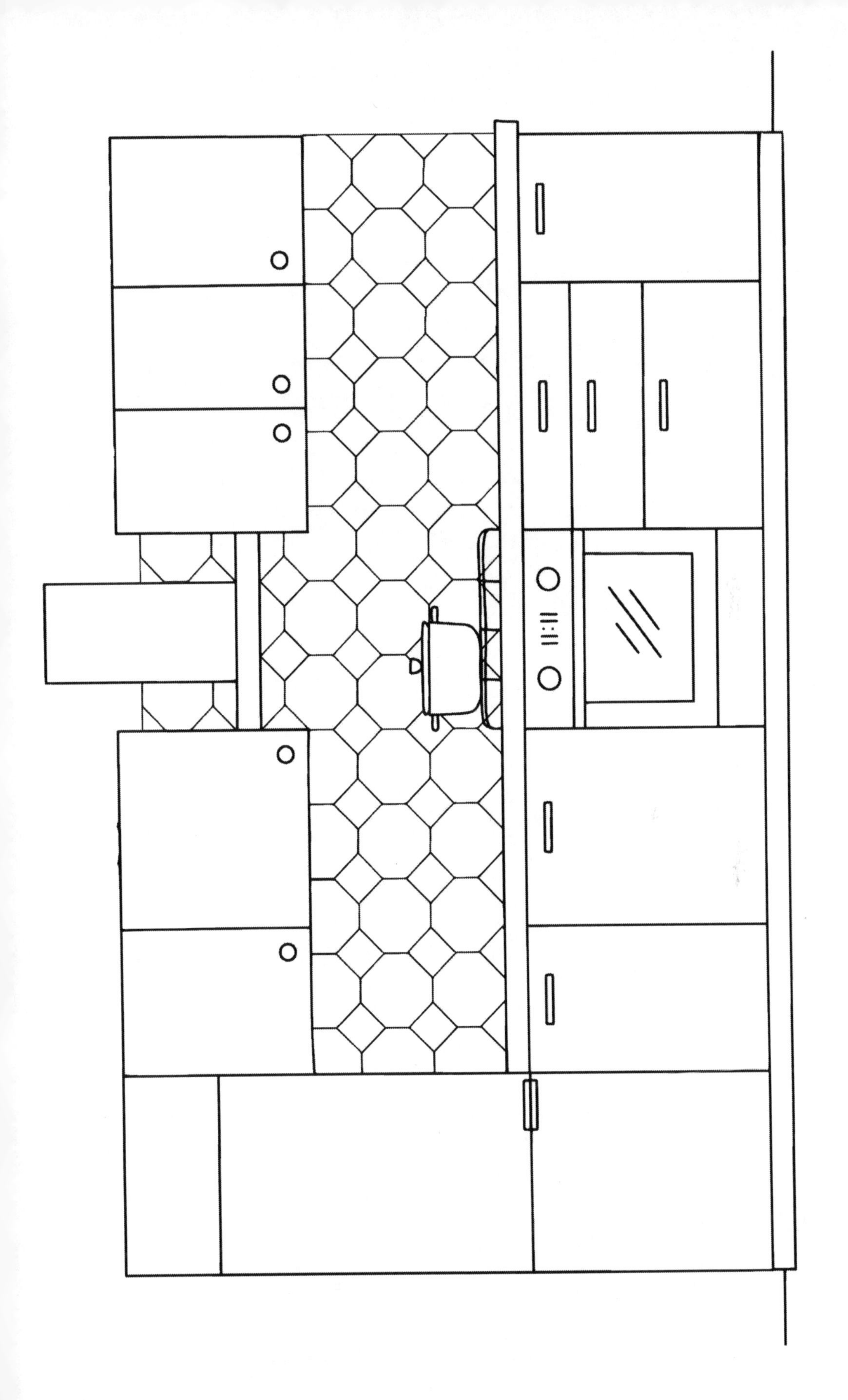

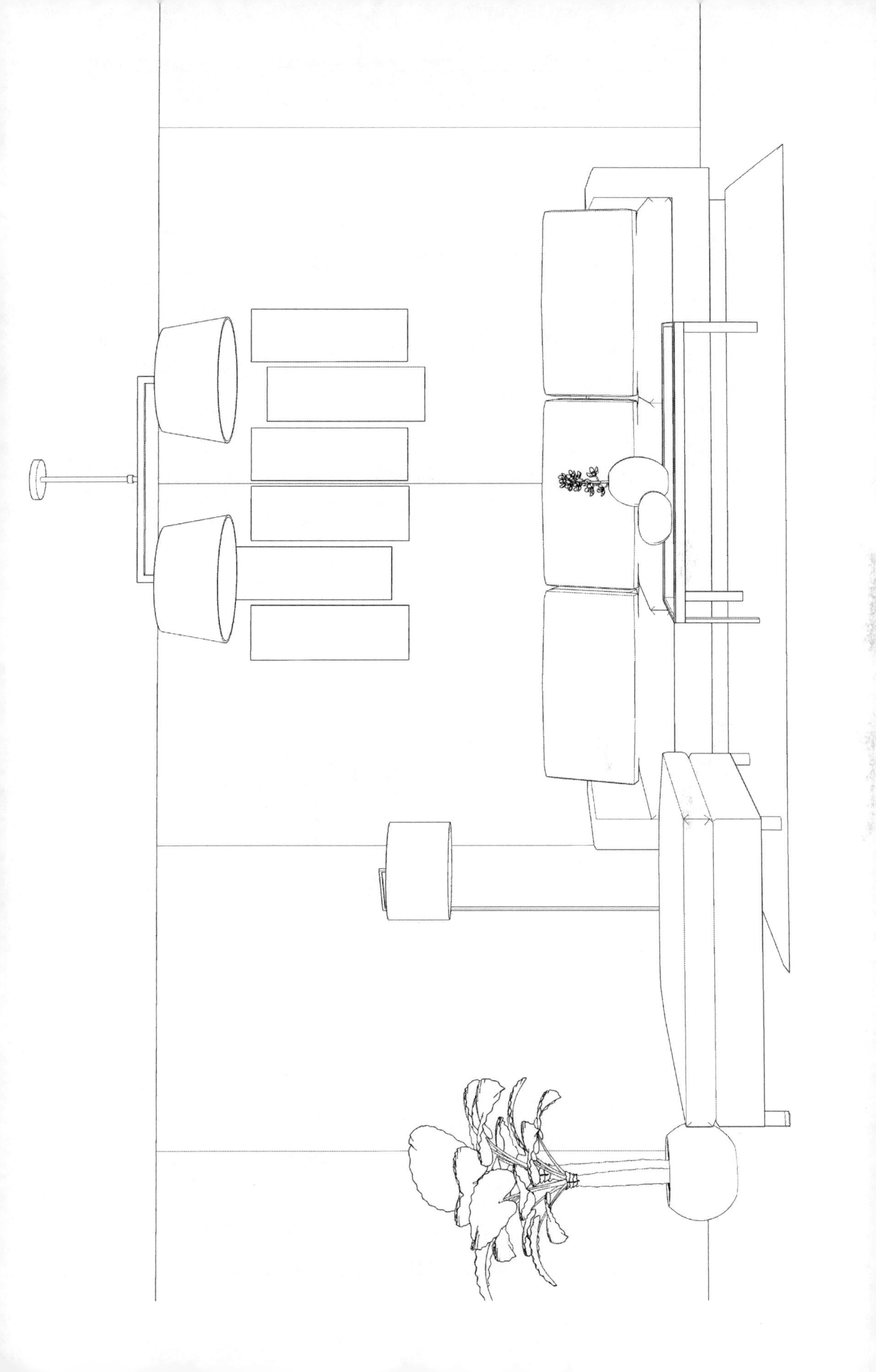

Puzzles

Directions to Solve a Logic Puzzle

1. To understand the puzzle clearly, carefully read the instructions.
2. Take note of any provided rules or clues.
3. If necessary, create a chart or grid to organize the information.
4. Use the clues to eliminate possibilities and narrow the available options.
5. Take your time and approach the puzzle in a step-by-step manner. Use your thinking skills to make sense of the information given to find the answers.

Directions for Crack the Code Puzzles

Determine the correct combination of three numbers for the lock using the clues given.

1. You will start with three digits.
2. Hints will indicate the accuracy of the digits.
3. Use the hints to figure out which numbers & number order will unlock the lock.
4. Once you have the correct code, you can open the lock.

Spot the differences

☐☐☐☐☐☐☐☐☐

Puzzle 1

Logic Puzzle #1

*Five friends, **Alice, Ben, Carla, Dan, and Emma**, were all born in different months of the year:
January, March, May, July, and September
*Each has a favorite color:
Blue, Green, Red, Yellow, and Purple
*Can you determine each friend's birth month and favorite color using the following clues?

- Emma was born in a month with the least amount of letters.
- Ben likes green. He wasn't born in July.
- Carla wasn't born in a month that starts with an M or J.
- The person born in January likes red.
- Dan was born in July or September.
- The person who likes yellow was born in July.
- Alice's birthday is before everyone else's.
- The person born in May likes blue.

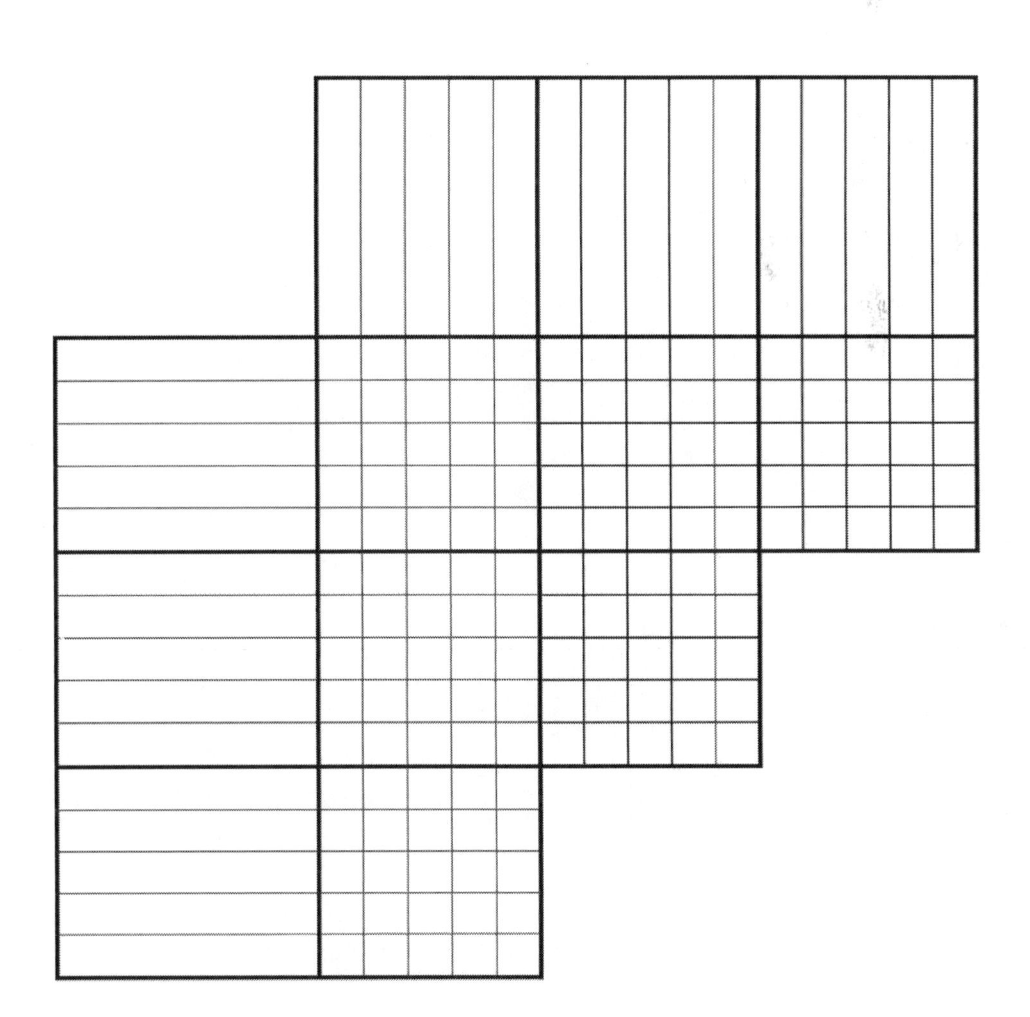

Crack the Code

Puzzle 1

5	8	1	One is correct but in the wrong spot
2	9	4	Nothing is correct
6	2	7	One is correct and in the right spot
9	7	5	Two are correct but both are in the wrong spot
3	9	5	Two are correct. One is in the wrong spot and one is in the right spot

___ ___ ___

Puzzle 2

7	2	1	One is correct but in the wrong spot
3	7	5	Nothing is correct
5	8	4	One is correct but in the wrong spot
4	9	2	Two are correct but both are in the wrong spot
7	1	6	One is correct and in the right spot
2	7	4	Two are correct. One is in the wrong spot and one is in the right spot.

___ ___ ___

Test your memory.

Study the image for one minute before turning the page.

Stop! View previous page first!

What two items are missing from the previous page?

Spot the differences

□□□□□□□□□

Puzzle 2

Logic Puzzle #2

*Five employees, **Angela, Dwight, Jim, Pam, and Stanley**, work at a paper company, and each has a different favorite drink:
Coffee, Soda, Tea, Water, and Juice
*Each has a different favorite color:
Blue, Green, Purple, Red, and Gray
*Can you determine each person's favorite drink and color using the clues below?

- Angela's favorite color is gray. She doesn't like juice or coffee.
- Dwight doesn't like soda. His drink has caffeine. His favorite color is not gray or red.
- Jim's favorite drink is soda. He doesn't like purple or red.
- Pam's favorite color is blue. She doesn't like tea.
- Stanley likes water. His favorite color is not purple or green.

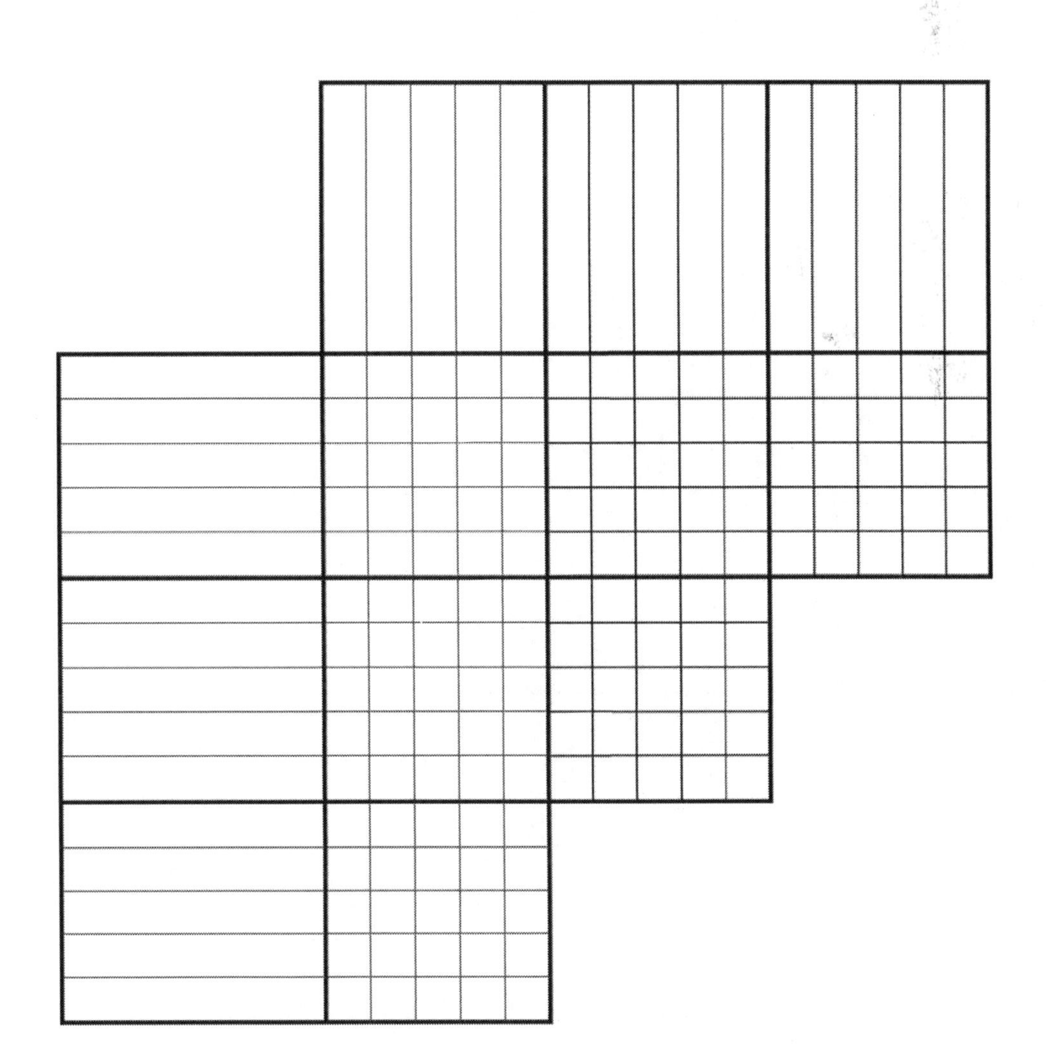

Crack the Code

Puzzle 3

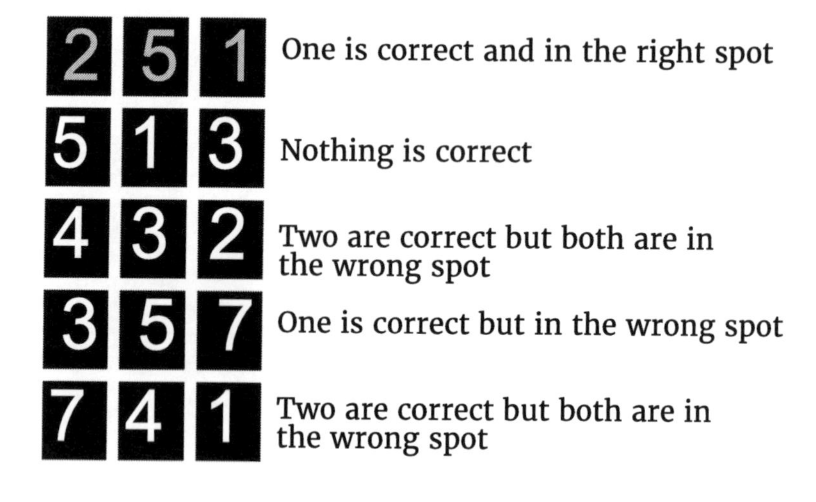

___ ___ ___

Puzzle 4

1	6	2	Two are correct and in the right spots
9	7	5	Nothing is correct
4	3	2	One is correct and in the right spot
1	8	3	One is correct but in the wrong spot
5	8	2	Two are correct. One in the right spot and one in the wrong spot

___ ___ ___

Test your memory.

Study the image for one minute before turning the page.

Stop! View previous page first!

What three items are missing from the previous page?

Spot the differences

□□□□□□□□

Puzzle 3

Logic Puzzle #3

*Five members of the Soprano family, **Tony, Silvio, Paulie, Christopher, and Bobby**, all have different code names: **Turtle, Spice, Pickle, Cat, and Bear**

*They drive different cars: **Cadillac, Corvette, Escalade, Ford, and Mercedes.**

*Can you determine each person's nickname and car using the clues below?

- Tony doesn't drive a Ford, Cadillac, or Mercedes. His nickname is not Cat.
- Silvio's nickname begins with the letter "S." He does not drive a Cadillac.
- Paulie's car is not a Ford or the Cadilac. His nickname is not Cat, but it is an animal.
- Christopher's nickname does not begin with the letter "P." He drives a Corvette.
- Bobby's car is not a Mercedes. His nickname is Turtle.

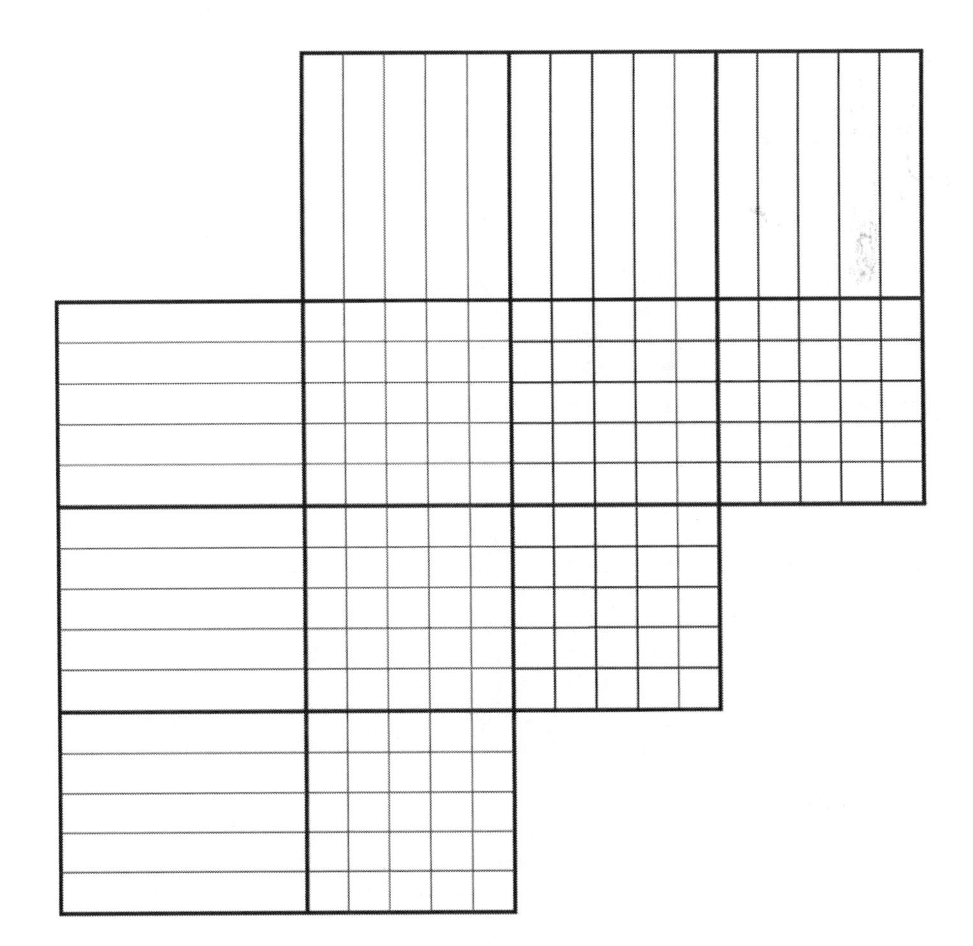

Crack the Code

Puzzle 5

9	6	3	One is correct but in the wrong spot
1	7	2	Nothing is correct
8	1	4	One is correct and is in the right spot
7	4	9	Two are correct but both are in the wrong spot
5	7	9	Two are correct. One is in the wrong spot and one is in the right spot

___ ___ ___

Puzzle 6

1	8	2	One is correct but in the wrong spot
6	1	4	Nothing is correct
4	9	5	One is correct but is in the wrong spot
5	7	8	Two are correct both are in the wrong spot
1	2	3	One is correct and in the right spot
8	1	5	Two are correct. One is in the wrong spot and one is in the right spot

___ ___ ___

Test your memory.

Study the image for one minute before turning the page.

Stop! View previous page first!

What three items are missing from the previous page?

Spot the differences

□□□□□□□□□

Puzzle 4

Logic Puzzle #4

***Finn, Jake, Princess Bubblegum, Marceline, and BMO** each compete in one of the following events:
Obstacle course, Sword Fighting, Archery, Video Gaming, and 50-yard dash.
*Each competitor is wearing a different colored outfit:
Green, Blue, Red, Yellow, and Purple.
*Using the clues below, can you determine which competitor competes in each event and what color outfit they wear?

- Princess Bubblegum is not wearing green or competing in the obstacle course. Her event does not involve running.
- Finn is wearing yellow and is not competing in the obstacle course or archery.
- Marceline is wearing green and is not competing in the archery event.
- BMO is competing in the video game tournament and is not wearing purple.
- Jake is wearing blue and is not competing in the archery event.
- The person wearing green is sword fighting.

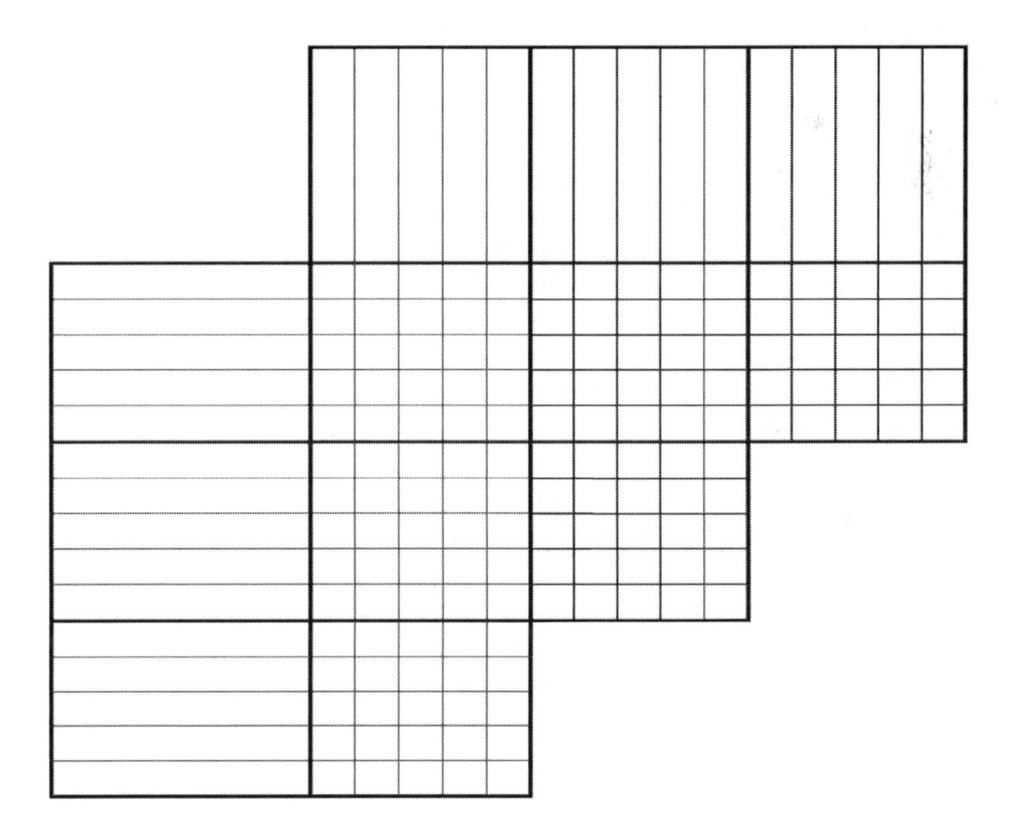

Crack the Code

Puzzle 7

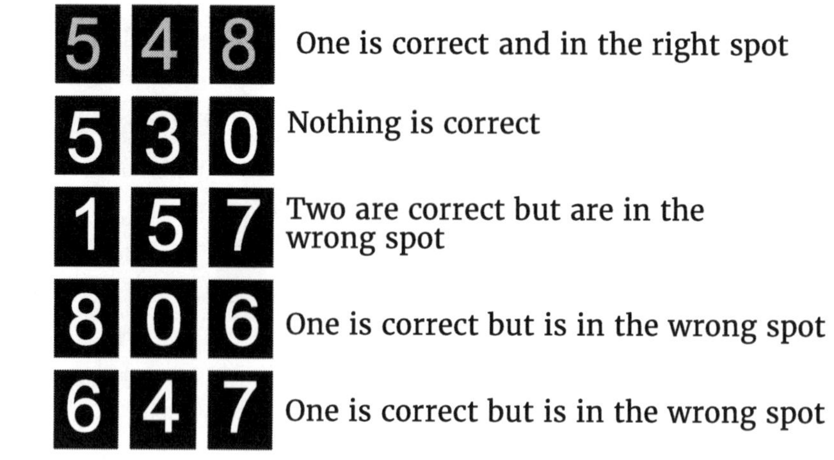

Puzzle 8

4	0	6	One is correct but is in the wrong spot
6	3	0	One is correct and is in the right spot
8	7	2	Two are correct but both are in the wrong spot
2	4	3	One is correct but is in the wrong spot
7	1	4	Nothing is correct

Test your memory.

Study the image for one minute before turning the page.

Stop! View previous page first!

What three items are missing from the previous page?

Spot the differences

□□□□□□□□□□□

Puzzle 5

Logic Puzzle #5

***Cartman, Kyle, Stan, Kenny, and Butters** play different video games at the South Park arcade.

*The games are: **Racing, Dancing, Fighting, Puzzles, and Music**

*The high scores are **300,400,500,700 and 800**

*Using the clues, can you determine the game each is playing and their high score?

- Cartman is playing the racing game and has a higher score than Stan and Kyle.
- Butters has the lowest score and is not playing fighting or puzzle games.
- Kyle is not playing puzzle or fighting games and has a higher score than Kenny.
- The person playing the dancing game has a higher score than the person playing the puzzle game but not higher than the racing game.
- The person playing the fighting game has a higher score than those playing the puzzle and music game.
- Kenny's score is better than only one other person's.
- Stan's score is in the middle, and he is not playing dancing, music, or puzzle games.

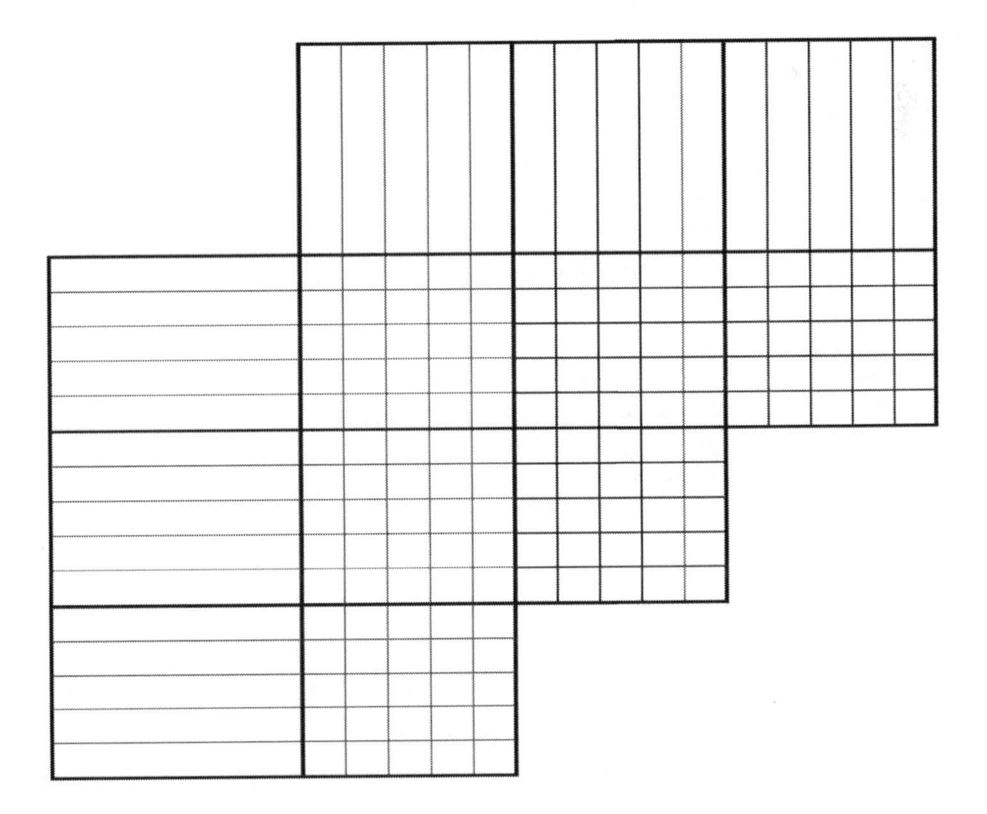

Crack the Code

Puzzle 9

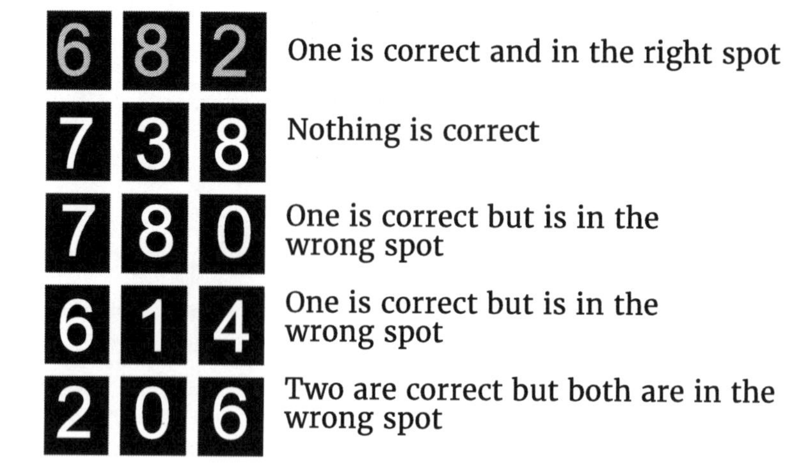

___ ___ ___

Puzzle 10

4	1	3	Two are correct. One in the wrong spot and one in the right spot
7	0	5	One is correct and in the right spot
1	0	7	Two are correct both are in the right spot
8	0	1	Two are correct one is in the right spot and one is in the wrong spot
9	8	2	Nothing is correct

___ ___ ___

Test your memory.

Study the image for one minute before turning the page.

Stop! View previous page first!

What three items are missing from the previous page?

Puzzle Answers

Group 1 Puzzle Answers

Spot the Difference Puzzle 1 Answer

Logic Puzzle #1 Answers

Alice - January - red
Ben - March - green
Carla - September - Purple
Dan - July - Yellow
Emma - May - Blue

Crack the Code Puzzle # 1 Answer

357

Crack the Code Puzzle # 2 Answer

246

Memory Answers

Girl with Pearl Earring: Johannes Vermeer

Group 2 Puzzle Answers

Spot the Difference Puzzle 2 Answer

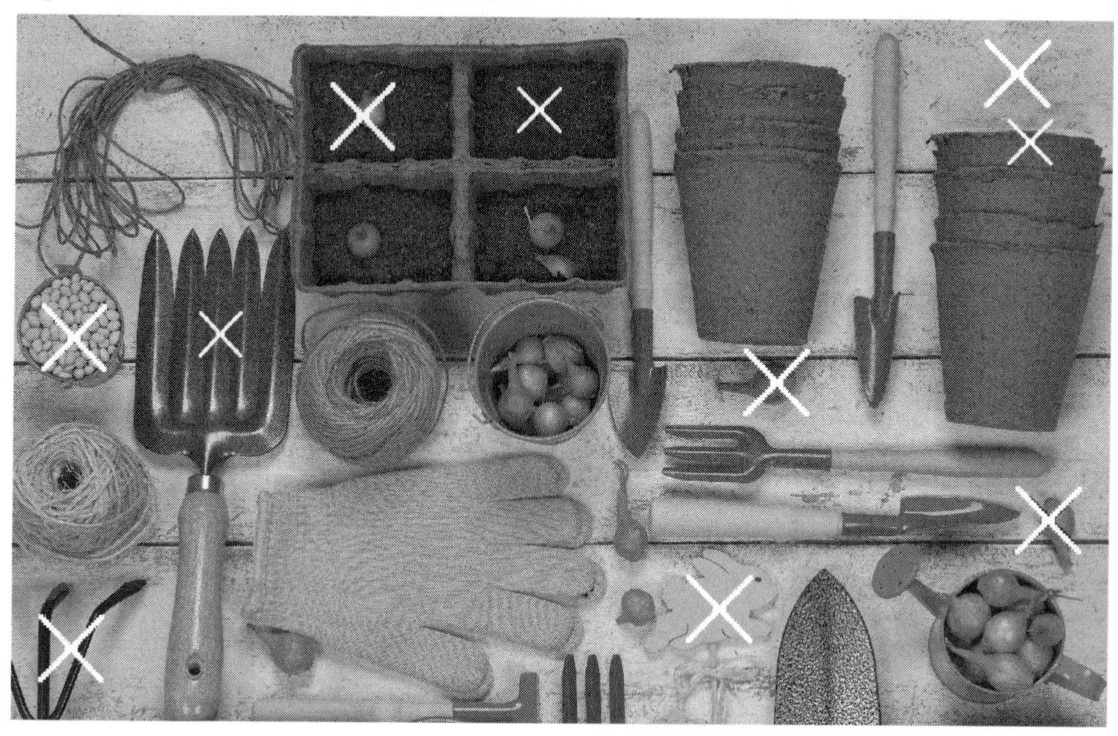

Logic Puzzle #2 Answers

Angela - Tea - Gray
Dwight - Coffee - Purple
Jim - Soda - Green
Pam -Juice - Blue
Stanley - Water - Red

Crack the Code Puzzle # 3 Answer

274

Crack the Code Puzzle # 4 Answer

862

Memory Answers

Mona Lisa: Leonardo da Vinci

Group 3 Puzzle Answers

Spot the Difference Puzzle 3 Answer

Logic Puzzle #3 Answers

Tony - Escalade - Pickle
Silvio - Ford - Spice
Paulie - Mercedes - Bear
Christopher - Corvette - Cat
Bobby - Cadillac - Turtle

Crack the Code Puzzle # 5 Answer

594

Crack the Code Puzzle # 6 Answer

853

Memory Answers

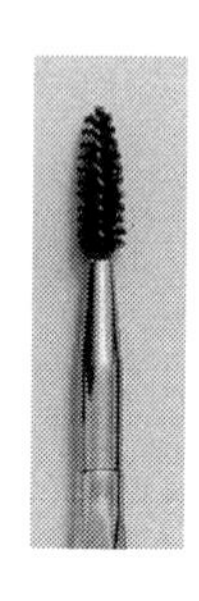

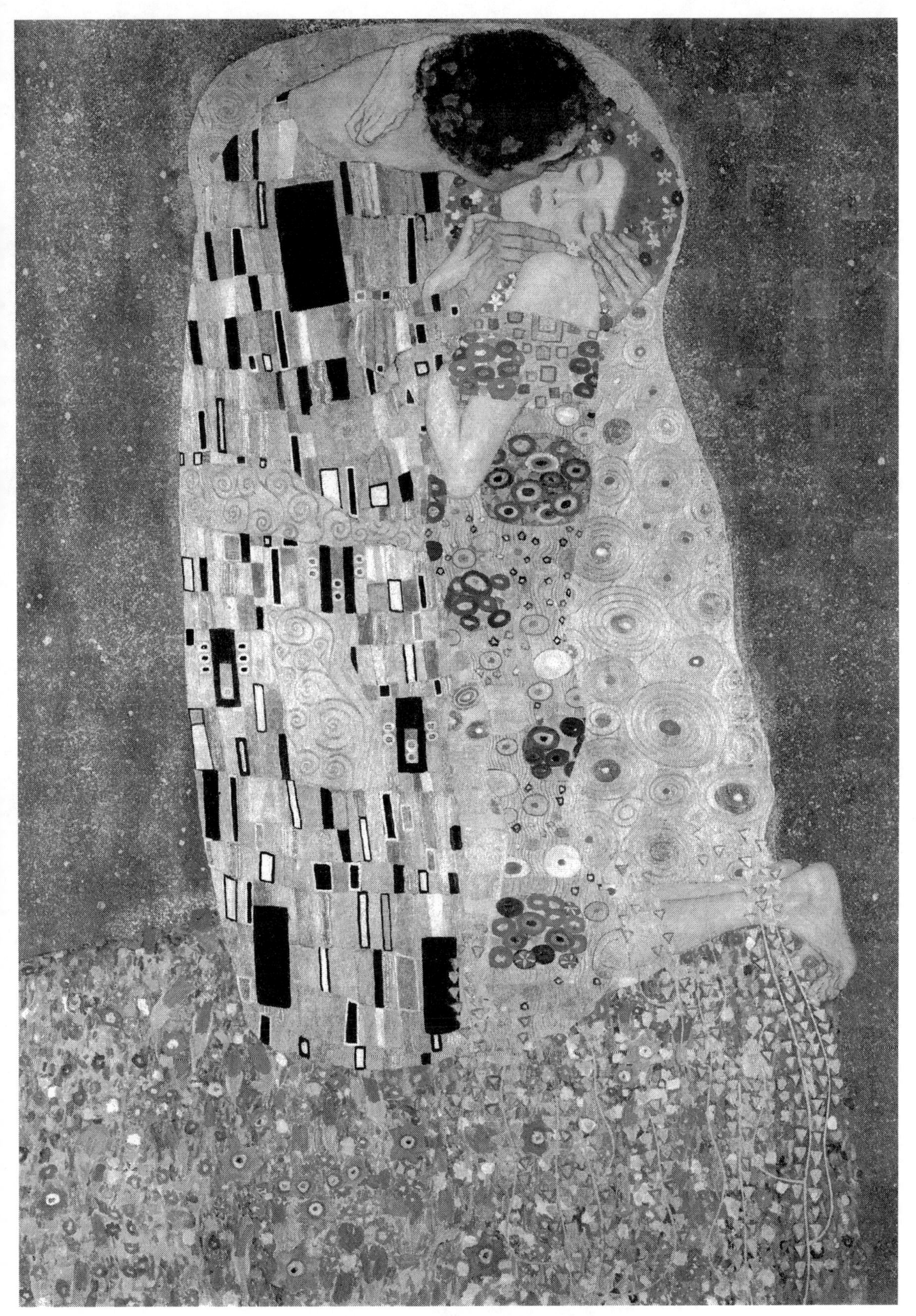

The Kiss: Gustav Klimt

Group 4 Puzzle Answers

Spot the Difference Puzzle 4 Answer

Logic Puzzle #4 Answers

Finn - Yellow - 50-yard-dash
Jake - Blue - Obstacle course
Princess Bubblegum - Purple - Archery
Marceline - Green - Sword fighting
BMO - Red - Video game tournament

Crack the Code Puzzle # 7 Answer

718

Crack the Code Puzzle # 8 Answer

628

Memory Answers

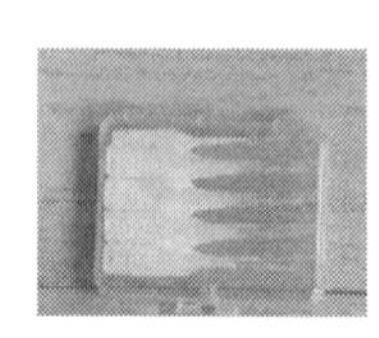

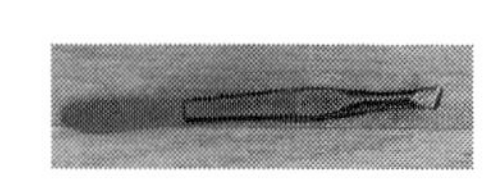

Two Sisters: Pierre-Auguste Renior

Group 5 Puzzle Answers

Spot the Difference Puzzle 5 Answer

Logic Puzzles #5 Answers

Cartman - Racing game - High score of 800
Kyle - Dancing game - High score of 700
Stan - Fighting game - High score of 500
Kenny - Puzzle game - High score of 400
Butters - Music game - High score of 300

Crack the Code Puzzle # 9 Answer

042

Crack the Code Puzzle # 10 Answer

103

Memory Answers

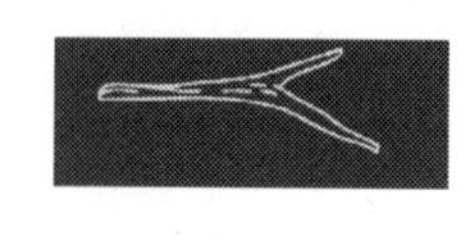

Two Owls: Julie de Graag

Lasagna – Submitted by Jeffrey Place

(makes two 5oz bowls)

Ingredients:

*12 oz sharp cheddar squeeze cheese (3/4 of a 16oz bottle)
*One 6 oz bag of beef crumbles or cooked ground beef
*One 12 oz bag of egg noodles
*One 3.5 oz bag of pepperoni slices
*Spices of choice
*One 4 oz block of mozzarella cheese
*One 15.5 oz bottle of pizza/spaghetti sauce
*Parmesan cheese

Preparation:

Pour pizza or spaghetti sauce into a medium bowl and season with spices. (I use 1t black pepper, 1t garlic salt/powder, 1 palm full of minced onion, and 1t of Dash seasoning blend) Fill the empty sauce bottle with water and pour it into the sauce. Stir together. Fill the squeeze cheese bottle with hot water and microwave until the cheese is liquefied. Put beef crumbles in the bowl and season as you like. Then microwave for 45 seconds.

Assembly:

In one large or two small bowls, put a 1-inch layer of egg noodles. Pour on the sauce until the noodles are covered. Add a layer of pepperoni and then sprinkle with beef. Add a layer of mozzarella cheese, and then pour a layer of liquefied squeeze cheese. Repeat with another layer of noodles, sauce, meats, mozzarella, and squeeze cheese. Finish with a heavy dusting of parmesan cheese.

Baking:

Microwave for 13 minutes on high. Remove and cover with a lid and wrap in a blanket, heavy towel, or coat. Let sit for a couple of hours to finish baking. Enjoy!

Frito Pie – Submitted by Michael Conway

Ingredients for 2 servings:

*6 oz white rice seasoned to taste with garlic and chili season packet from ramen soup
*3 oz summer sausage (use half the sausage per serving)
*Four 10" Tortilla Shells (2 per serving)
*11.25 oz Chili (with or without beans)
*7 slices of pepperoni
*12 oz BBQ Corn Chips
*8 oz tub of jalapeno or mild cheese
*BBQ sauce

Assembly:

In a 6-7 oz bowl, place 1 tortilla shell to cover the bottom and sides. Add cooked seasoned rice to the bowl, spreading around evenly. Put cut-up sausage on top of the rice and cover that with corn chips. Put spoonfuls of cheese on several areas of the chips. Pour chili over the chips and spread around until all chips are covered. Put the second tortilla shell on top of the chili, poking it down the sides of the bowl until it looks like the top of a pie. Spread a layer of cheese on top, and then add pepperoni slices. Squirt several lines of bbq sauce on top. Microwave for 2 ½ - 3 minutes. Enjoy!

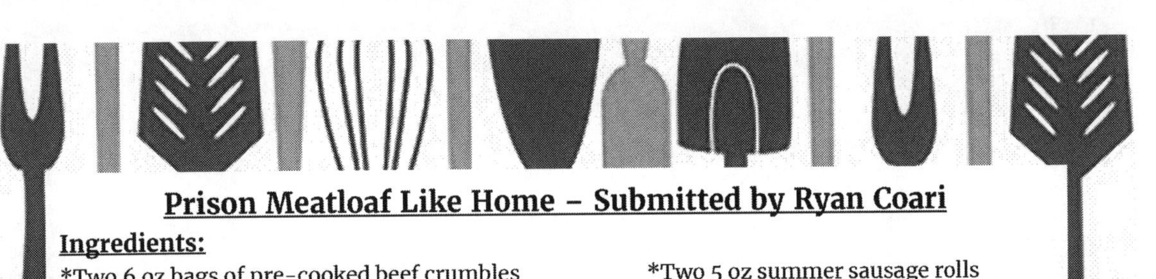

Prison Meatloaf Like Home – Submitted by Ryan Coari

Ingredients:

*Two 6 oz bags of pre-cooked beef crumbles
*One 4 oz mozzarella cheese stick, grated
*Minced dried onion
*Black Pepper
*Ketchup
*Two 5 oz summer sausage rolls
*One sleeve of butter crackers
*Sea Salt
*Garlic Powder
*Mrs. Dash (optional)

Assembly:

Start by taking the skin off of the summer sausage and mash up the sausage until it is the consistency of ground beef. Mix the summer sausage, beef crumbles, onion, spices, and 3/4 sleeve of crackers together in a large bag. (Tortilla chip bag works great) Mix until the meat forms a ball. Form into a loaf. Scoop out a section of the middle of the loaf, forming a well. Squirt inside the well with ketchup. Add half of the grated cheese to the well and more minced onion. Form the scooped-out portion of the meat into a patty and place it on top, filling in the well and leaving no space around it. Add a little more ketchup to the top, sprinkle with more minced onion, Mrs. Dash, and the rest of the grated cheese.

Cook in the microwave for 12 minutes on high. Let it cool and enjoy!

No Egg, No Bake Cheesecake – Submitted by David M. Castaldi

Ingredients:

*8 oz Non-dairy powdered creamer
*16 oz pack of duplex cookies
*Strawberries or strawberry preserves (optional)
*10 oz soft cream cheese
*3/4 stick of butter
*Chocolate chips (optional)

Assembly:

Scrap the icing from the cookies into a bowl, placing cookies in a separate bowl. Once all cookies are scraped, add cream cheese to the icing bowl and microwave for 2-3 minutes until smooth.

Smash cookies into crumbs. Melt butter and add to cookie crumbs and stir together. Add crumbs to a 9x9x4 cake pan and press evenly into the bottom, forming a crust. Take microwaved cream cheese mixture and add powdered creamer and mix well. Microwave for a minute or two at a time until the mixture becomes smooth with a spoon. Dump mixture onto cookie crumbs and spread evenly.

Place in refrigerator or freezer for 30-60 minutes to set up. Add the strawberry topping of your choice and top with chocolate chips if desired. Enjoy!

The Card Players: Paul Cezanne

Traditional Solitaire

Number of players: 1
Deck: A standard deck of 52 playing cards
Aim: The goal of Solitaire is to build four foundation piles in ascending order from Ace to King, one for each suit (hearts, diamonds, clubs, spades).
Set-up:

- Start by shuffling a standard deck of 52 playing cards.
- Deal out 28 cards into seven tableau piles. The first pile should have one card face-up, the second pile should have two cards (one face-down and one face-up), the third pile should have three cards (two face-down and one face-up), and so on. The remaining cards are placed in a stockpile facedown.

Game Play:

- Begin by examining the top card of the seven piles. You can move cards between tableau piles following these rules:
    - You can move a face-up card onto a tableau pile if it's one rank lower and of the opposite color. For example, you can move a red 7 onto a black 8.
    - You can move a group of face-up cards in sequence onto another tableau pile if they follow the same color and descending order. For instance, you can move a sequence of black 9, red 8, and black 7 onto a red 10.
    - If a tableau pile becomes empty, you can move a King (or a King with a group of cards) from any pile to fill the space.
- Utilize the stockpile and waste pile:
    - When you don't have any more moves on the tableau, you can turn over cards from the stockpile to the waste pile. You can play the top card of the waste pile onto the tableau or foundation piles following the regular rules.
    - Once the stockpile is empty, you can turn over the waste pile and use it as the new stockpile, reshuffling it if necessary.
- Build the foundation piles:
    - As you uncover Aces in the tableau, you can move them to start the foundation piles (you will have four foundation piles). From there, you can build on each foundation pile in ascending order, following the suit.

End of game:

- The game is won when you successfully move all cards to the foundation piles, completing each pile from Ace to King in the same suit.

California Speed

Number of players: 2
Deck: A standard deck of 52 playing cards
Aim: To be the first player to get rid of all your cards.
Set-Up:

- Shuffle the cards.
- Each player will receive half the deck, or 26 cards exactly.
- Players will receive their cards facedown, take them into their hands as a pile, and keep them facedown, preventing their opponent and themselves from viewing any of the cards.

Card Rankings and Values:

- Ranking and suits do not matter.
- The only thing players will look for is matching sets.

Gameplay:

- Once both players have their piles in hand, the game can begin.
- Simultaneously both players will flip the top card of their pile face up onto the table in front of them. This will be done four times so that each player has a line of 4 cards in front of them.
- Once the last card for each player is placed, players can start to search for matching sets.
- A match consists of two to four cards of the same value, for example, three 4s or two Aces.
- When a player spots a match, they will deal cards from their piles face up to cover all the matching cards.
- If both players spot a match at the same time, they will be racing to cover the cards faster.
- Both players may end up covering cards in the match but cannot cover the same card together.
- If the new cards create more matches, players will continue to cover up cards with cards from their hands.
- This continues until there are no more valid matches to cover.
- Each player will now collect all the cards stacked on the four piles in front of them and add them to the bottom of their pile.
- Once cards are situated back in the pile, players will start to deal out 4 cards face up in front of themselves and repeat the gameplay as above.
- This continues until a player plays out the final card from their pile onto a match to the faceup cards in front of either player. The full match does not need to be covered just as long as one of the valid cards of a match is.

End of Game:

- The game ends when a player empties their hand. They are the winner of the game.

Crazy Eights

Number of players: 2 or more
Deck: A standard deck of 52 playing cards
Aim: To be the first player to get rid of all your cards.
Set-Up:

- Shuffle the deck and deal 5 cards to each player.
- Place the remaining cards facedown in a draw pile.
- Flip the top card of the draw pile face-up next to it. This card will be the starting card for the discard pile.

Game Play:

- The player to the left of the dealer goes first. They must play a card that matches either the suit or rank of the top card in the discard pile. For example, if the top card is a 7 of hearts, they can play any heart card or any other 7 from their hand.
- If a player cannot play a card that matches the suit or rank, they must draw a card from the draw pile. If they can play the drawn card, they can do so. Otherwise, their turn ends.
- If a player has an "8" card, they can play it regardless of the suit or rank of the top card. When playing an "8", the player must also declare the suit that the next player must match. For example, if a player plays an 8 of spades, they can choose the suit to be spades, and the next player must play a spade or another 8.
- The game continues clockwise, with each player trying to play a card that matches the suit or rank of the top card in the discard pile.
- If a player doesn't have any playable cards, they must draw from the draw pile until they get a card they can play. If the draw pile runs out, reshuffle the cards in the discard pile (excluding the top card) to create a new draw pile.

End of game:

- The first player to get rid of all their cards is the winner. The game can continue for additional rounds if desired.

Optional variations:

- Some variations allow players to stack cards of the same rank on top of each other, causing the next player to draw multiple cards.
- Another variation allows players to play multiple cards of the same rank at once. For example, if the top card is a 10 of clubs, a player can play two or more 10s at once.
- Remember to clarify any specific house rules or variations before starting the game. Have fun playing Crazy Eights!

Kings on the Corners

Number of players: 2 - 4
Deck: A standard deck of 52 playing cards
Aim: To be the first player to get rid of all your cards.
Set-up:

- Deal seven cards to each player.
- Place the remaining cards in the middle of the table.
- Turn the four top cards over, placing one on each of the four sides of the deck.

Game Play:

- The player to the dealer's left begins by drawing one card from the center pile.
- The player may make as many valid plays as possible during his turn to get rid of as many cards as possible from his hand.
- Once there are no more valid moves, it's the next player's turn.
- Each player begins their turn by drawing a card from the center pile and making as many valid moves as possible.

Valid moves:

- Play a card (or sequence of cards) on one of the cards that has been turned over. To play cards on a foundation pile, the card played must be immediately below the first card in rank and of the opposite color (red or black). For example, if a 9♥ is on the foundation pile, the next card face played must be 8♣ or 8♠. You can play as many cards as possible as long as it follows the rule of the opposite color going down. Ace is the last card that can be played.
- Play a "King in the Corner." Kings are the only cards that can be played in the corner spaces created by the cross. Once a King is played, players may lay cards on that pile following the rules of the foundation piles.
- Move an entire foundation pile onto another pile if the bottom card of that recipient pile and the top card of the moving pile creates a valid sequence. This is often possible when the cards are first dealt.
- Play any card or sequence of cards on a vacated foundation pile.
- If you want to track scores across multiple games, there are different ways to do it. You can keep score based on the number of cards remaining, the total value of the remaining cards, or by assigning each card a point value except for the Kings, which are worth ten points.

End of game:

- The winner is the first player to get rid of all their cards.

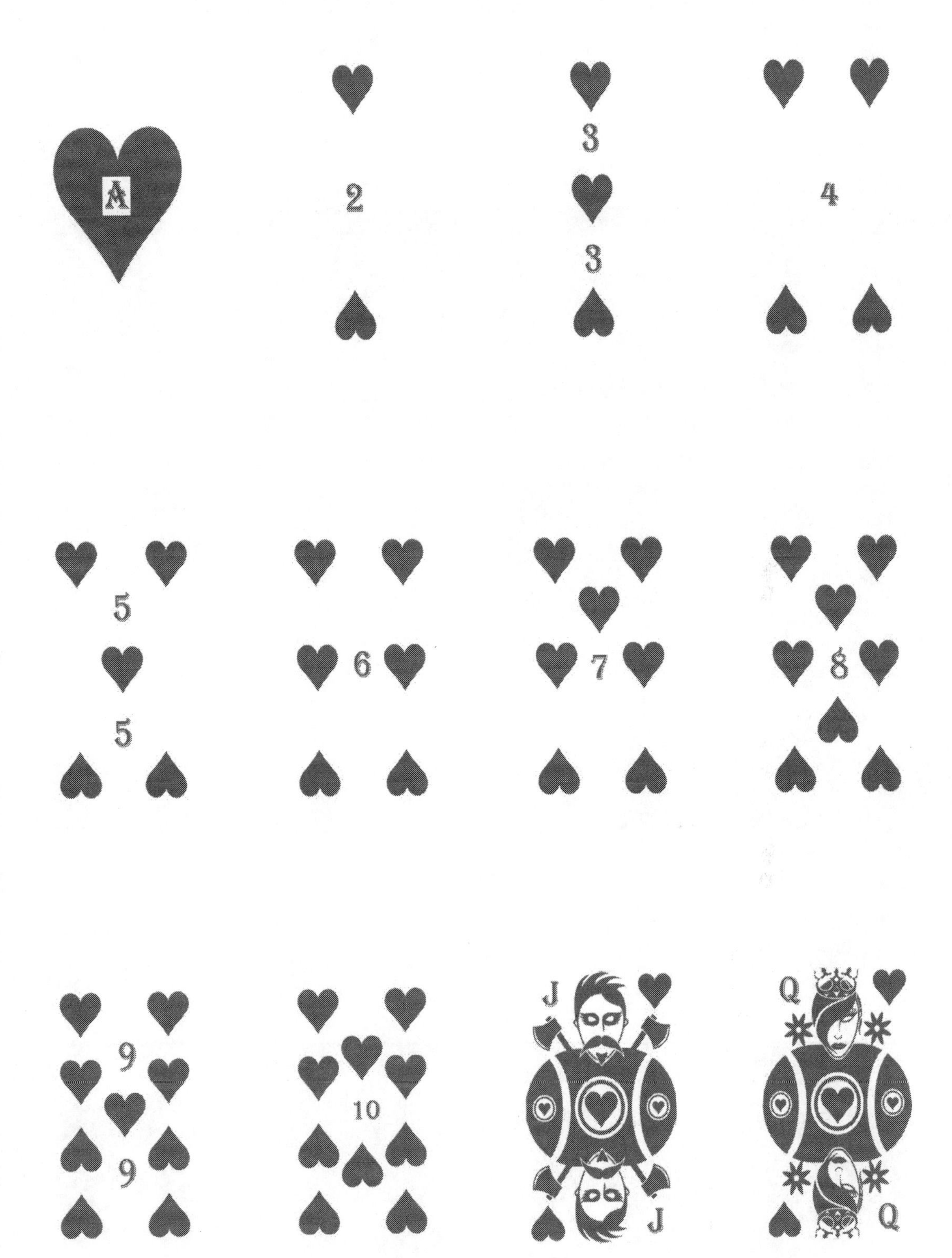

A

2

3
3

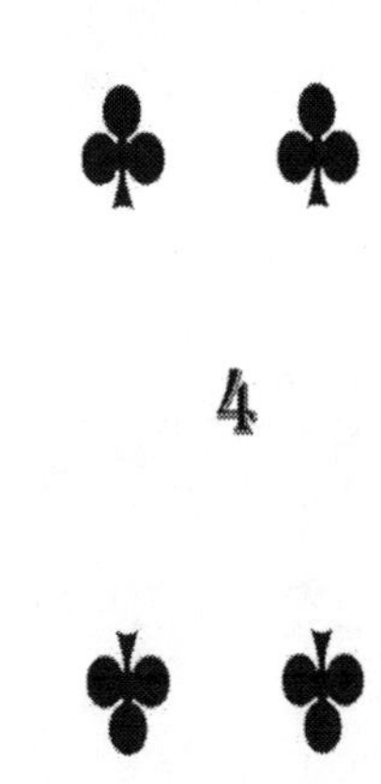
4

5
5

6

7

8

9
9

10

J
J

Q

A
2
3
3
4
5
5
6
7
8
9
9
10
J
J
Q
Q

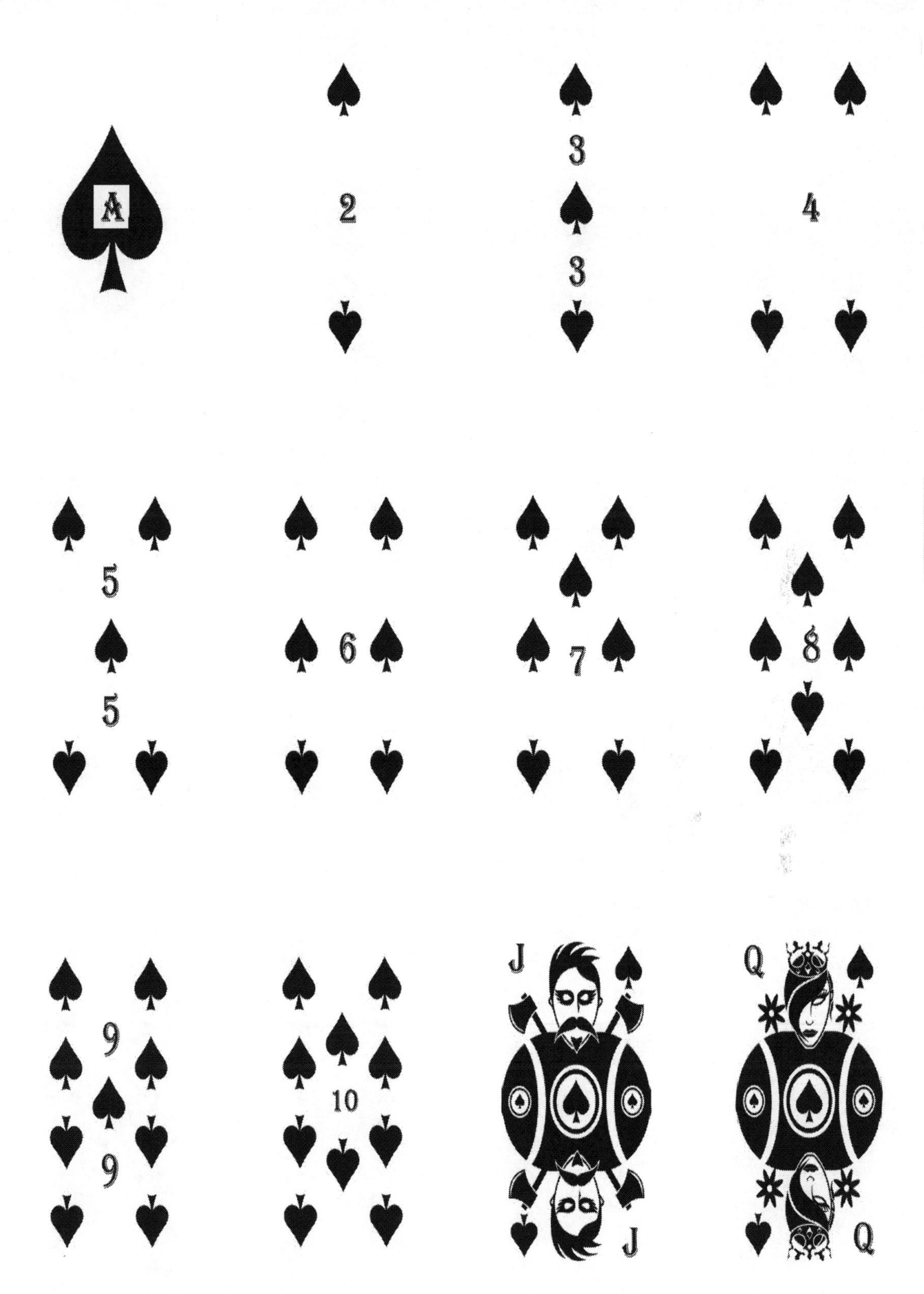
A
2
3
3
4
5
5
6
7
8
9
9
10
J
J
Q
Q

K
K

JOKER

K
K

JOKER

K
K

JOKER

K
K

JOKER

2024

January

S	M	T	W	T	F	S
	1	2	3	4	5	6
7	8	9	10	11	12	13
14	15	16	17	18	19	20
21	22	23	24	25	26	27
28	29	30	31			

February

S	M	T	W	T	F	S
				1	2	3
4	5	6	7	8	9	10
11	12	13	14	15	16	17
18	19	20	21	22	23	24
25	26	27	28	29		

March

S	M	T	W	T	F	S
					1	2
3	4	5	6	7	8	9
10	11	12	13	14	15	16
17	18	19	20	21	22	23
24	25	26	27	28	29	30
31						

April

S	M	T	W	T	F	S
	1	2	3	4	5	6
7	8	9	10	11	12	13
14	15	16	17	18	19	20
21	22	23	24	25	26	27
28	29	30				

May

S	M	T	W	T	F	S
			1	2	3	4
5	6	7	8	9	10	11
12	13	14	15	16	17	18
19	20	21	22	23	24	25
26	27	28	29	30	31	

June

S	M	T	W	T	F	S
						1
2	3	4	5	6	7	8
9	10	11	12	13	14	15
16	17	18	19	20	21	22
23	24	25	26	27	28	29
30						

July

S	M	T	W	T	F	S
	1	2	3	4	5	6
7	8	9	10	11	12	13
14	15	16	17	18	19	20
21	22	23	24	25	26	27
28	29	30	31			

August

S	M	T	W	T	F	S
				1	2	3
4	5	6	7	8	9	10
11	12	13	14	15	16	17
18	19	20	21	22	23	24
25	26	27	28	29	30	31

September

S	M	T	W	T	F	S
1	2	3	4	5	6	7
8	9	10	11	12	13	14
15	16	17	18	19	20	21
22	23	24	25	26	27	28
29	30					

October

S	M	T	W	T	F	S
		1	2	3	4	5
6	7	8	9	10	11	12
13	14	15	16	17	18	19
20	21	22	23	24	25	26
27	28	29	30	31		

November

S	M	T	W	T	F	S
					1	2
3	4	5	6	7	8	9
10	11	12	13	14	15	16
17	18	19	20	21	22	23
24	25	26	27	28	29	30

December

S	M	T	W	T	F	S
1	2	3	4	5	6	7
8	9	10	11	12	13	14
15	16	17	18	19	20	21
22	23	24	25	26	27	28
29	30	31				

2025

January

S	M	T	W	T	F	S
			1	2	3	4
5	6	7	8	9	10	11
12	13	14	15	16	17	18
19	20	21	22	23	24	25
26	27	28	29	30	31	

February

S	M	T	W	T	F	S
						1
2	3	4	5	6	7	8
9	10	11	12	13	14	15
16	17	18	19	20	21	22
23	24	25	26	27	28	

March

S	M	T	W	T	F	S
						1
2	3	4	5	6	7	8
9	10	11	12	13	14	15
16	17	18	19	20	21	22
23	24	25	26	27	28	29
30	31					

April

S	M	T	W	T	F	S
		1	2	3	4	5
6	7	8	9	10	11	12
13	14	15	16	17	18	19
20	21	22	23	24	25	26
27	28	29	30			

May

S	M	T	W	T	F	S
				1	2	3
4	5	6	7	8	9	10
11	12	13	14	15	16	17
18	19	20	21	22	23	24
25	26	27	28	29	30	31

June

S	M	T	W	T	F	S
1	2	3	4	5	6	7
8	9	10	11	12	13	14
15	16	17	18	19	20	21
22	23	24	25	26	27	28
29	30					

July

S	M	T	W	T	F	S
		1	2	3	4	5
6	7	8	9	10	11	12
13	14	15	16	17	18	19
20	21	22	23	24	25	26
27	28	29	30	31		

August

S	M	T	W	T	F	S
					1	2
3	4	5	6	7	8	9
10	11	12	13	14	15	16
17	18	19	20	21	22	23
24	25	26	27	28	29	30
31						

September

S	M	T	W	T	F	S
	1	2	3	4	5	6
7	8	9	10	11	12	13
14	15	16	17	18	19	20
21	22	23	24	25	26	27
28	29	30				

October

S	M	T	W	T	F	S
			1	2	3	4
5	6	7	8	9	10	11
12	13	14	15	16	17	18
19	20	21	22	23	24	25
26	27	28	29	30	31	

November

S	M	T	W	T	F	S
						1
2	3	4	5	6	7	8
9	10	11	12	13	14	15
16	17	18	19	20	21	22
23	24	25	26	27	28	29
30						

December

S	M	T	W	T	F	S
	1	2	3	4	5	6
7	8	9	10	11	12	13
14	15	16	17	18	19	20
21	22	23	24	25	26	27
28	29	30	31			

2026

January

S	M	T	W	T	F	S
				1	2	3
4	5	6	7	8	9	10
11	12	13	14	15	16	17
18	19	20	21	22	23	24
25	26	27	28	29	30	31

February

S	M	T	W	T	F	S
1	2	3	4	5	6	7
8	9	10	11	12	13	14
15	16	17	18	19	20	21
22	23	24	25	26	27	28

March

S	M	T	W	T	F	S
1	2	3	4	5	6	7
8	9	10	11	12	13	14
15	16	17	18	19	20	21
22	23	24	25	26	27	28
29	30	31				

April

S	M	T	W	T	F	S
			1	2	3	4
5	6	7	8	9	10	11
12	13	14	15	16	17	18
19	20	21	22	23	24	25
26	27	28	29	30		

May

S	M	T	W	T	F	S
					1	2
3	4	5	6	7	8	9
10	11	12	13	14	15	16
17	18	19	20	21	22	23
24	25	26	27	28	29	30
31						

June

S	M	T	W	T	F	S
	1	2	3	4	5	6
7	8	9	10	11	12	13
14	15	16	17	18	19	20
21	22	23	24	25	26	27
28	29	30				

July

S	M	T	W	T	F	S
			1	2	3	4
5	6	7	8	9	10	11
12	13	14	15	16	17	18
19	20	21	22	23	24	25
26	27	28	29	30	31	

August

S	M	T	W	T	F	S
						1
2	3	4	5	6	7	8
9	10	11	12	13	14	15
16	17	18	19	20	21	22
23	24	25	26	27	28	29
30	31					

September

S	M	T	W	T	F	S
		1	2	3	4	5
6	7	8	9	10	11	12
13	14	15	16	17	18	19
20	21	22	23	24	25	26
27	28	29	30			

October

S	M	T	W	T	F	S
				1	2	3
4	5	6	7	8	9	10
11	12	13	14	15	16	17
18	19	20	21	22	23	24
25	26	27	28	29	30	31

November

S	M	T	W	T	F	S
1	2	3	4	5	6	7
8	9	10	11	12	13	14
15	16	17	18	19	20	21
22	23	24	25	26	27	28
29	30					

December

S	M	T	W	T	F	S
		1	2	3	4	5
6	7	8	9	10	11	12
13	14	15	16	17	18	19
20	21	22	23	24	25	26
27	28	29	30	31		

2027

January

S	M	T	W	T	F	S
					1	2
3	4	5	6	7	8	9
10	11	12	13	14	15	16
17	18	19	20	21	22	23
24	25	26	27	28	29	30
31						

February

S	M	T	W	T	F	S
	1	2	3	4	5	6
7	8	9	10	11	12	13
14	15	16	17	18	19	20
21	22	23	24	25	26	27
28						

March

S	M	T	W	T	F	S
	1	2	3	4	5	6
7	8	9	10	11	12	13
14	15	16	17	18	19	20
21	22	23	24	25	26	27
28	29	30	31			

April

S	M	T	W	T	F	S
				1	2	3
4	5	6	7	8	9	10
11	12	13	14	15	16	17
18	19	20	21	22	23	24
25	26	27	28	29	30	

May

S	M	T	W	T	F	S
						1
2	3	4	5	6	7	8
9	10	11	12	13	14	15
16	17	18	19	20	21	22
23	24	25	26	27	28	29
30	31					

June

S	M	T	W	T	F	S
		1	2	3	4	5
6	7	8	9	10	11	12
13	14	15	16	17	18	19
20	21	22	23	24	25	26
27	28	29	30			

July

S	M	T	W	T	F	S
				1	2	3
4	5	6	7	8	9	10
11	12	13	14	15	16	17
18	19	20	21	22	23	24
25	26	27	28	29	30	31

August

S	M	T	W	T	F	S
1	2	3	4	5	6	7
8	9	10	11	12	13	14
15	16	17	18	19	20	21
22	23	24	25	26	27	28
29	30	31				

September

S	M	T	W	T	F	S
			1	2	3	4
5	6	7	8	9	10	11
12	13	14	15	16	17	18
19	20	21	22	23	24	25
26	27	28	29	30		

October

S	M	T	W	T	F	S
					1	2
3	4	5	6	7	8	9
10	11	12	13	14	15	16
17	18	19	20	21	22	23
24	25	26	27	28	29	30
31						

November

S	M	T	W	T	F	S
	1	2	3	4	5	6
7	8	9	10	11	12	13
14	15	16	17	18	19	20
21	22	23	24	25	26	27
28	29	30				

December

S	M	T	W	T	F	S
			1	2	3	4
5	6	7	8	9	10	11
12	13	14	15	16	17	18
19	20	21	22	23	24	25
26	27	28	29	30	31	

2028

January

Su	Mo	Tu	We	Th	Fr	Sa
						1
2	3	4	5	6	7	8
9	10	11	12	13	14	15
16	17	18	19	20	21	22
23	24	25	26	27	28	29
30	31					

February

Su	Mo	Tu	We	Th	Fr	Sa
		1	2	3	4	5
6	7	8	9	10	11	12
13	14	15	16	17	18	19
20	21	22	23	24	25	26
27	28	29				

March

Su	Mo	Tu	We	Th	Fr	Sa
			1	2	3	4
5	6	7	8	9	10	11
12	13	14	15	16	17	18
19	20	21	22	23	24	25
26	27	28	29	30	31	

April

Su	Mo	Tu	We	Th	Fr	Sa
						1
2	3	4	5	6	7	8
9	10	11	12	13	14	15
16	17	18	19	20	21	22
23	24	25	26	27	28	29
30						

May

Su	Mo	Tu	We	Th	Fr	Sa
	1	2	3	4	5	6
7	8	9	10	11	12	13
14	15	16	17	18	19	20
21	22	23	24	25	26	27
28	29	30	31			

June

Su	Mo	Tu	We	Th	Fr	Sa
				1	2	3
4	5	6	7	8	9	10
11	12	13	14	15	16	17
18	19	20	21	22	23	24
25	26	27	28	29	30	

July

Su	Mo	Tu	We	Th	Fr	Sa
						1
2	3	4	5	6	7	8
9	10	11	12	13	14	15
16	17	18	19	20	21	22
23	24	25	26	27	28	29
30	31					

August

Su	Mo	Tu	We	Th	Fr	Sa
		1	2	3	4	5
6	7	8	9	10	11	12
13	14	15	16	17	18	19
20	21	22	23	24	25	26
27	28	29	30	31		

September

Su	Mo	Tu	We	Th	Fr	Sa
					1	2
3	4	5	6	7	8	9
10	11	12	13	14	15	16
17	18	19	20	21	22	23
24	25	26	27	28	29	30

October

Su	Mo	Tu	We	Th	Fr	Sa
1	2	3	4	5	6	7
8	9	10	11	12	13	14
15	16	17	18	19	20	21
22	23	24	25	26	27	28
29	30	31				

November

Su	Mo	Tu	We	Th	Fr	Sa
			1	2	3	4
5	6	7	8	9	10	11
12	13	14	15	16	17	18
19	20	21	22	23	24	25
26	27	28	29	30		

December

Su	Mo	Tu	We	Th	Fr	Sa
					1	2
3	4	5	6	7	8	9
10	11	12	13	14	15	16
17	18	19	20	21	22	23
24	25	26	27	28	29	30
31						

2029

January

Su	Mo	Tu	We	Th	Fr	Sa
	1	2	3	4	5	6
7	8	9	10	11	12	13
14	15	16	17	18	19	20
21	22	23	24	25	26	27
28	29	30	31			

February

Su	Mo	Tu	We	Th	Fr	Sa
				1	2	3
4	5	6	7	8	9	10
11	12	13	14	15	16	17
18	19	20	21	22	23	24
25	26	27	28			

March

Su	Mo	Tu	We	Th	Fr	Sa
				1	2	3
4	5	6	7	8	9	10
11	12	13	14	15	16	17
18	19	20	21	22	23	24
25	26	27	28	29	30	31

April

Su	Mo	Tu	We	Th	Fr	Sa
1	2	3	4	5	6	7
8	9	10	11	12	13	14
15	16	17	18	19	20	21
22	23	24	25	26	27	28
29	30					

May

Su	Mo	Tu	We	Th	Fr	Sa
		1	2	3	4	5
6	7	8	9	10	11	12
13	14	15	16	17	18	19
20	21	22	23	24	25	26
27	28	29	30	31		

June

Su	Mo	Tu	We	Th	Fr	Sa
					1	2
3	4	5	6	7	8	9
10	11	12	13	14	15	16
17	18	19	20	21	22	23
24	25	26	27	28	29	30

July

Su	Mo	Tu	We	Th	Fr	Sa
1	2	3	4	5	6	7
8	9	10	11	12	13	14
15	16	17	18	19	20	21
22	23	24	25	26	27	28
29	30	31				

August

Su	Mo	Tu	We	Th	Fr	Sa
			1	2	3	4
5	6	7	8	9	10	11
12	13	14	15	16	17	18
19	20	21	22	23	24	25
26	27	28	29	30	31	

September

Su	Mo	Tu	We	Th	Fr	Sa
						1
2	3	4	5	6	7	8
9	10	11	12	13	14	15
16	17	18	19	20	21	22
23	24	25	26	27	28	29
30						

October

Su	Mo	Tu	We	Th	Fr	Sa
	1	2	3	4	5	6
7	8	9	10	11	12	13
14	15	16	17	18	19	20
21	22	23	24	25	26	27
28	29	30	31			

November

Su	Mo	Tu	We	Th	Fr	Sa
				1	2	3
4	5	6	7	8	9	10
11	12	13	14	15	16	17
18	19	20	21	22	23	24
25	26	27	28	29	30	

December

Su	Mo	Tu	We	Th	Fr	Sa
						1
2	3	4	5	6	7	8
9	10	11	12	13	14	15
16	17	18	19	20	21	22
23	24	25	26	27	28	29
30	31					

Create heartfelt connections with
your personalized greeting cards,
where each carefully crafted message
becomes a unique expression of love,
celebration, or appreciation.

Created with care by:

I LOVE YOU
BEARY MUCH!

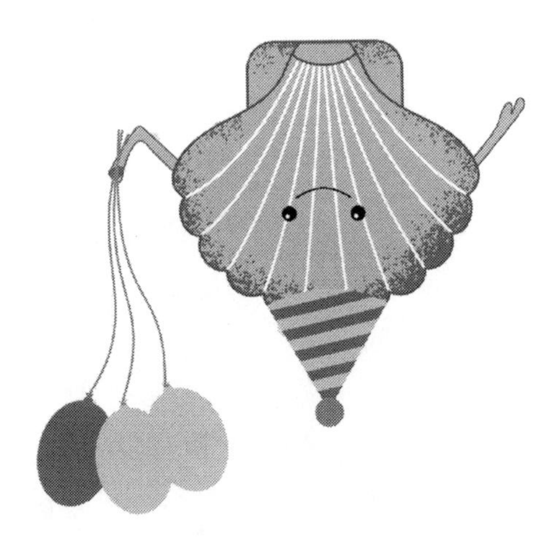

Created with care by:

HAPPY BIRTHDAY

LET'S SHELL-EBRATE!

HAPPY
Birthday
TO YOU!

Created with care by:

You are paw-some

Made With Love By:

Happy Birthday

Enjoy your day

Created by:
with love

happy
Valentines
day

Hugs and kisses

Created with care by:

Wishing the best dad
an amazing day!

Created with love by:

Created with care by:

Get Well Soon

Created with love by:

HAPPY HOLIDAYS

BE

Merry

AND

Bright

Created with love by:

miss you

Created with care by:

MY HEART BEATS FOR YOU

Happy
Mother's
Day

I LOVE YOU MOM!
THANKS FOR EVERYTHING!

Created with love by:

Created with love by:
Thinking of you

Thank You!

First and foremost, we would like to express our gratitude to Mr. Larry Emerson, Jeffrey Place, Ryan Coari, David M. Castaldi, and Michael Conway. They graciously compiled their commissary recipes, which we proudly present in this book. Thank you!

Thank you to Kelly Brotzman, Executive Director, Prison Book Program, Quincy, MA. Her unwavering commitment to improving the lives of people who are incarcerated and her enthusiasm for sharing knowledge and books is instrumental in improving the lives of many. Her efforts have ensured our books reach those who can benefit from them the most. Thank you!

A special mention goes to Lori Branigan, whose attention to detail and meticulous efforts ensured that the puzzles in this book are accurate and enjoyable. Thank you!

To our readers,

We understand that many of you have received our inmate activity book as a gift from a loved one. Your perspective on the book is invaluable, and we kindly ask you to talk with the person who gifted it. Share your thoughts on the activities, their impact on your well-being, and how they've helped you pass the time. Discuss the aspects of the book that have helped you the most. Your words have the potential to inspire and guide others who may be seeking constructive outlets during their incarceration.

We ask that you encourage your loved ones to leave an honest review on platforms such as Amazon or Barnes & Noble. These reviews provide valuable feedback for us as creators and assist potential readers in making informed decisions about the book's potential impact on their loved ones.

We express our deepest appreciation for your support and for being part of our prison activity book community. Your feedback is of immeasurable value to us, and we eagerly await your reviews.

Thank you for your time, and may this book continue to be a source of inspiration and growth during your time incarcerated.

Sincerely,
Beth and Patricia